Leaving Laodicea

*How to Find the Wisdom You Need to
Survive the Days Ahead*

A 21 Day Devotional

Steve McCranie

A Back2Acts Production

Leaving Laodicea

How to Find the Wisdom You Need to Survive the Days Ahead

Published by Back2Acts Productions.
ISBN-13: 9780977155835
ISBN-10: 0977155838

Leaving Laodicea may be purchased in bulk for educational, business, fundraising, or sales promotion use. For information, please contact: info@Back2Acts.com.

For additional Leaving Laodicea resources, including free downloads, please visit our website: www.leavinglaodicea.com.

Printed in the United States of America

15 16 17 18 19 20

To Karen McCranie

My wife, my companion, and my best friend.

"It's been quite a ride, hasn't it?"

"Those who don't know history are destined to repeat it."

— Edmund Burke

"The only thing we learn from history is that we learn nothing from history."

— Georg Wilhelm Friedrich Hegel

CONTENTS

A QUICK WORD

A prudent man foresees evil and hides himself,
But the simple pass on and are punished.
Proverbs 22:3

LET ME BE DIRECT FROM THE START. We are living in troubling times. For those of us in the west, these are unparalleled times in the history of our nation.

Just look around. Almost every day we are bombarded with another story of racial or political tension that is tearing at the very fabric of our nation. We have the constant fear of terrorism, both at home and abroad, that lingers in the back of the minds of many today. There's the threat of another financial crisis, much like the crisis of 2008, or worse yet, a repeat of 1929 that looms just over the horizon. Corruption in our sacred institutions is almost epidemic. There's little trust in the principles that our nation was founded upon: "Life, liberty, and the pursuit of happiness." Instead, "every man does what is right in his own eyes" (Judges 21:25) with little thought of how it impacts others.

Yes, we are truly living in troubling times.

If any nation deserves the judgment of God, it's certainly ours. The Supreme Court has now legalized and legitimized the sin of homosexuality— something the Scriptures clearly call an "abomination" (Lev. 18:22), and our courts are now beginning to punish those who dare to think otherwise. We have the blood of 80 million unborn children on our hands, yet the church has done little, if anything, to "deliver those who are drawn toward death, and hold back those stumbling to the slaughter" (Prov. 24:11). Why? Because we're too busy building our own lives and fortunes and accumulating all our trinkets and toys to be concerned about what God is concerned about.

I say this to our collective shame.

How has all this happened? How did we allow this to take place under our watch? How did it get *so* bad *so* fast?

The Lord, speaking about the time before His coming, said "because lawlessness (wickedness) will abound, the love of *many* will grow cold" (Matt. 24:12). The *many* Jesus was speaking about also includes the church, the bride of Christ— yes, even you and me.

Jesus said that those living in the last church age, in the time right before His return, would be characterized by worldliness and lukewarmness— so much so that it would make Jesus sick. That's right. The church in the Laodicean age would literally make Him sick to the point of vomiting (Rev. 3:16).

Our view of the church and His view of us are not the same. We think we've got it all together with our hyped praise bands, multi-campus mega-churches, and our hip, relevant pastors. But Jesus sees the church differently.

> **Revelation 3:15-16** - "I know your works, that you are neither cold nor hot. I could wish you were cold or hot. So then, because you are lukewarm, and neither cold nor hot, I will *vomit you out of My mouth*."

Why does the church in Laodicea make Jesus feel this way? It's because our view of church and His view of His bride have very little in common. He continues:

> **Revelation 3:17** - "Because *you say* (our view), 'I am rich, have become wealthy, and have need of nothing'— and *do not know* (His view) that you are wretched, miserable, poor, blind, and naked."

Jesus' words to His church get even worse:

> **Revelation 3:20** - "Behold, I stand at the door and knock. If anyone hears My voice and opens the door, I will come in to him and dine with him, and he with Me."

Where is Jesus standing? What door is He knocking on? For years the church has spiritualized these words to mean the "door of our heart" or "opening our heart to let Jesus in" to bring salvation. Stop and read the verse in context. This has nothing to do with salvation. The door Jesus is talking about is the door of the church. Jesus is on the *outside* of His church knocking and asking us, His bride, to let Him in.

Again, I say all of this to our great shame.

Leaving Laodicea

What are we to do? How can we forsake the lukewarm, apathetic, sickening life of Laodicea and embrace true Christianity, the "faith which was once for all delivered to the saints" (Jude 1:3)? How can we grow deep in our faith experience with Him in order to face the storms coming our way?

Please understand that what might have worked in the past simply won't work today. An anemic, children's church Jesus will not be enough for you to survive what is soon to take place in our land of Laodicea. A preschool, flannel graph faith will not sustain you when the clouds of judgment begin to swirl. You need more. We all need more.

That's the purpose of this book.

Over the next few weeks you and I are going to dig deep into the first few verses of Proverbs, God's glorious book of wisdom, and glean what it means to "know wisdom and instruction, and to perceive the words of understanding" (Prov. 1:2). We're going to slow down and take our time discovering all God has for us in these few verses. Wisdom is ours for the asking (James 1:5). It's a gift given to His church by the sacrifice of Christ and the indwelling presence of the Holy Spirit (1 Cor. 1:30). So it's worth committing some of our precious time to discover exactly what God's wisdom truly means.

What you are holding in your hands is hopefully more than just a simple Bible Study or Daily Devotional. Its core design is to help you dive deep into the book of Proverbs to discover true wisdom, and then show you how to appropriate that wisdom into your own life.

Getting Serious and the Next Step Challenge

These daily studies are somewhat long compared to most popular devotionals. They're not designed to be read in 15 minutes or during a quick coffee break. Each chapter ends with a section of questions titled **Getting Serious** to help you do just that about the things of God. The deeper you journey into this book, the more difficult the questions become. These questions are personal and probing and you will be encouraged to reflect honestly on each one before moving on to the next. Don't skip this part. This is where you will strive to make His Word personal and binding. And this is where spiritual growth will take place.

After that, the **Next Step Challenge** is designed to provide you with some tools for digging deeper into the Word in order to help you glean more than what you might be used to doing. I would plan for at least an hour, or maybe two, to complete each chapter. Even then, we haven't even scratched the surface of all God has in these few verses.

Come What May

Finally, I want to personally thank you for taking the time with me to delve deeper into the book of Proverbs and to seek the wisdom of God above all else. I pray God will reveal His incredible presence in your life as you go through these chapters, like He did with me as I wrote them.

Will you join me as we endeavor to experience Leaving Laodicea together? Will you come with me on this journey to be more like Christ? And will you accompany me as we both strive to leave the apathy and lukewarmness of Laodicea behind forever, no matter what, come what may?

PREFACE

The Coming Darkness

"You know how to discern the face of the sky, but you cannot discern the signs of the times."

Matthew 16:3

A S WE EMBARK ON THIS JOURNEY together, I want to begin by showing you the reason we need to spend time— even more time than we've ever done in the past— to study God's Word and dig deep into His wisdom granted to us by virtue of His Son. It was Jesus alone who "became for us wisdom from God— and righteousness and sanctification and redemption" (1 Cor. 1:30).

Let's begin with a bit of a reality check, shall we? Let's look at the current cultural situation in our nation as it actually is. Let's take the blinders off, see the times in which we live, and consider why it's so vitally important to spend the time and make the sacrifices necessary to acquire the wisdom of God.

After all, as the Proverbs say: "*Wisdom* is the principal thing; therefore get *wisdom*" (Prov. 4:7).

Reality Check

On Friday, June 26, 2015, the Supreme Court ruled that homosexual couples have the right to marry nationwide, thus establishing a new civil right in our land. In effect, by their 5-4 decision, five unelected lawyers redefined the meaning of the word "marriage" and forever changed the landscape for Christians, and the church, in this country.

What has been historically deemed as deviant behavior by our society, and a sin and an abomination by the Bible and the church, is now the law of the land. Those who oppose this law will be guilty of violating the law. Soon the full force and weight of the State will come against those who hold uncompromisingly to biblical values and a biblical worldview in an effort to crush them and bring them into submission and compliance. The door is now wide open for full-scale persecution of the church in America. Unfortunately, most believers have their head buried neck deep in the sand hoping that this is a bad dream that will soon go away.

Wish again. The nightmare is here and it's here to stay.

Dred Scott v. Sandford and Roe v. Wade

This is not the first time the Supreme Court made an infamous ruling and defiantly shook its fist in the face of God. In 1857, the Dred Scott v. Sandford decision essentially stripped African Americans of their right of personhood and relegated them to the status of a mere possession, or slave. It took a bloody

Civil War and the Emancipation Proclamation by President Abraham Lincoln to correct and set right the wrong the Supreme Court had decreed.

Still, the evil and injustice of this ruling, as reprehensible as it was, was not forcibly imposed upon Christians and the church. As Christians, we had the right and the duty to follow the clear teachings of Scripture and our own conscience. We could, and did, reject the ruling by treating people of color the same way we would treat each other.

Then, on January 22, 1973, in Roe v. Wade and Doe v. Bolton, the Supreme Court again ruled against God and basic human dignity when they denied unborn babies the rights of personhood and life. They held, by a 7 to 2 vote, that a woman's right to privacy and choice trumps an unborn child's right to life.

Consequently, 80 million unborn children have died.

But again, Christians in this country were not forced, under penalty of law, to participate or even endorse abortion. We had the freedom and the responsibility to speak for those who could not speak for themselves (Prov. 31:8), and to stand against this horrific holocaust. The church did just that, by the thousands. Crisis Pregnancy Centers sprang up all over the land, as well as homes for unwed mothers and the like.

Obergefell v. Hodges

This time, the Supreme Court ruling is different. With the Obergefell v. Hodges decision, gay marriage and the homosexual lifestyle has now been elevated to the lofty position of a civil right. To speak against it, like Christians did in the Dred Scott and Roe v. Wade decisions, is now tantamount to a crime— a potential hate crime.

Unlike in the past, this ruling *has* been forcefully imposed on the Christian and the church. It has become the law of the land, cast in judicial stone.

The civil rights of a legally protected class of sins now supersedes the religious liberty of the majority of Americans. The application of this ruling, in real time, will be the attempt to govern and control all speech about homosexuality that is contrary to the ruling. Anything deemed politically incorrect, anything that speaks against the recent ruling, and anything that offends the sensibility and well-being of the homosexual community will be smacked with the label of "intolerant, homophobic, hate speech." This means that our cherished freedom of speech will soon be subservient to the civil rights of a protected homosexual minority.

How will this affect each of us?

There are now passages in the Bible that our courts have ruled as potential hate speech because they offend the civil rights of a protected minority. Those who feel otherwise will soon be stripped of their rights to speak in the public square, to share their opinions or sincerely held convictions openly, and to worship anywhere but in the solitude and privacy of their own closets. In the view of the courts, we have no choice but to comply. The acceptance of homosexuality and gay marriage is now settled law.

It's the new law of the land.

It will soon be a hate crime for a preacher in a local church to accurately teach what the Bible says about homosexuality. And if he does, watch out! Defiance of the law of the land always comes with unwanted consequences.

In effect, the courts have now taken the battle to us and are forcing us to take a stand. We must choose whose law we will obey.

If we obey man's law and compromise and capitulate to the legal perversion set before us, we can probably live relatively quiet and peaceful lives. On the other hand, if we stand for biblical truth and commit, like our Lord, to being light in darkness (John 1:5), we will certainly find ourselves at odds with Caesar, and we will soon discover what persecution tastes like.

I know many of you might reject what I'm about to say, but I see Christians in America in the same place as the Jews found themselves in 1935, in Nazi Germany. Yes, you heard me right. I see us as living in Nazi Germany in 1935.

The parallels are striking.

This decision shows us clearly that the rule of law in America is dead. The Supreme Court now changes law to push its own agenda and has become, like the Executive and Legislative branches of our government, compromised and untrustworthy. In essence, the Republic we've all come to love and respect is no more. It has been replaced by those who will twist and manipulate the law and media to fit their own desired end. Widespread corruption, habitual lying, and dishonesty in the highest places of all three branches of our government leave us distressed as citizens of this great country.

The same thing happened to the citizens of Germany in the early 30's. They also saw their sacred institutions: the church, the school, the family, and the government hijacked and taken over by unscrupulous, evil men who would stop at nothing to achieve their selfish ends.

The result was World War II. Over 60 million people, amounting to over 3% of the earth's population at that time, died. The atrocities against the Jews were utterly unthinkable— until we discovered the ovens of Dachau, Auschwitz and Ravensbruck.

That Could Never Happen to Us in America

Why? Because we're better or more loving or more tolerant than the citizens of Germany? Open your eyes and look around. Read the headlines. Do you see a sense of civility and tolerance towards the church today? Have you read the vile and vicious comments made by the various citizens of this country against those who hold, for example, a biblical view of marriage? Do you trust your president to do what is honorable and right according to the law? Let's not forget Benghazi, the IRS targeting of conservative groups, the ATF and their "Fast and Furious" scheme, among countless others? And, of course, there are the cover ups and almost criminal delays in trying to get the government to honor congressional subpoenas or freedom of information requests from others trying to get to the bottom of all these scandals.

Do you believe that persecution is coming?

Listen to what a few notable voices say about the recent ruling and the chilling effect it will have on Christians and those who hold to a traditional view of marriage.

> "The majority attempts, toward the end of its opinion, to reassure those who oppose same-sex marriage that their rights of conscience will be protected. We will soon see whether this proves to be true. I assume that those who cling to old beliefs will be able to whisper their thoughts in the recesses of their homes, but if they repeat those views in public, they will risk being labeled as bigots and treated as such by governments, employers, and schools."

Supreme Court Justice Samuel Alito
in his Dissenting Opinion

"I think we're going to see persecution in this country. You better be ready and you better be prepared because it's coming. I think there will be persecution of Christians for our stand."

Evangelist Franklin Graham
Samaritan's Purse

"I believe a barrage of court cases has already been planned against those who hold to politically incorrect views of marriage. Many of us will be dragged into court to be prosecuted or subjected to civil judgments. Some will lose their jobs, while others forfeit their businesses. Some will be persecuted and ridiculed and fined. Some may go to prison as the years unfold. Since same-sex marriage has now been determined to be a universal human right by the highest court in the land, it will trump religious liberty, churches, seminaries, Christian schools, businesses and a host of individual liberties. I also fear judgment will befall this once great nation."

Dr. James Dobson
Focus on the Family and Family Talks

Don't be naive or deceived. Persecution will come, and it will come quickly. To reiterate, we are basically living in Nazi Germany in 1935.

The church would do well to remember what that means.

Edmund Burke once said, "Those who don't know history are destined to repeat it."

Georg Wilhelm Friedrich Hegel also said, almost prophetically, "The only thing we learn from history is that we learn nothing from history."

Let that not be said of the church today, and let that not be said of you and me.

Therefore Get Wisdom

More than ever, we need the Lord's wisdom. We need His wisdom to know how to stand in the midst of hard times. We need His wisdom to be able to clearly hear His voice speaking to us, as He has to countless others facing similar persecution over the centuries. And we need His wisdom to know how to bring Him glory, no matter what, come what may.

"*Wisdom* is the principal thing; therefore get *wisdom*" (Prov. 4:7).

Join me in discovering the depths of wisdom found only in God's Word. Let's begin our journey into the book of Proverbs.

INTRODUCTION

Finishing Dead Last

The proverbs of Solomon the son of David, king of Israel.
Proverbs 1:1

THE BOOK OF PROVERBS contains some of the over 3,000 sayings of Solomon (1 Kings 4:32), who is known as the wisest man who ever lived. Unfortunately, Solomon didn't always heed his own advice and found his life, family, and testimony shipwrecked in the end. By trusting in political expedience, rather than the Word of God, Solomon thought he could secure the kingdom that God had given to him through human, man-centered, sinful means. He married pagan wives in the hope of forging treaties and trade alliances with Israel's natural enemies. Slowly, Solomon's love of his Lord slipped away as he gave into the pagan demands of his 700 wives and 300 concubines (1 Kings 11:3).

Yes, you read that right. Solomon had 700 wives and 300 concubines. Just so we'll be on the same page, a concubine is the same thing as a wife, but not quite as special. A *concubine* could be defined as: Wife, Second Class. Solomon had at least 1,000 women in his life continually demanding his time and attention. As their husband, it was his job to make them happy, or at least *try* to make them happy.

How would Solomon, or you or me for that matter, make 1,000 women happy? Simple. You give them what they want.

Think practically for a moment. If Solomon spent just one evening with each of his wives and concubines, it would take him almost three years to have dinner with them all. That's assuming he didn't have one or two he liked more than the others. That's also assuming he never booked a wife for a second dinner date or took a day off to go fishing with the guys. The jealousy and infighting among these women for Solomon's attention and favors must have been fierce.

So Solomon foolishly gave into their constant nagging and let them do what they wanted to do, including serving and worshiping the foreign gods they brought with them from home. In doing so, Solomon let down his guard, forsook his role as the spiritual leader of his home, and let the enemy of God breach the walls of the sanctity of his life. He gave up on the most important duty entrusted to a man: to lead his family in the fear and admonition of the Lord (Eph. 6:4). "If you want to worship Baal, fine. Just don't bother me about it. I had a really nice time with you tonight and I'll see you again in a couple of years."

I ask myself, "How could a man who's supposed to be so wise do something so stupid?" Yet I've found myself making some of the same mistakes Solomon did. Has this ever happened to you?

Think about it.

Solomon willingly forgot about the Lord's warning to each of us regarding "light and darkness" and "being unequally yoked" (2 Cor. 6:14). He ignored the warning that says, "Do not be mislead (deceived), *bad company* corrupts *good character*" (1 Cor. 15:33 NIV). The *bad company* was the foreign gods Solomon allowed, not only into his kingdom, but also into his home. The *good character* was Solomon himself. He allowed himself to be corrupted by the evil influences in his life.

There's a lesson here for each of us.

Starting Strong, Finishing Weak

Solomon didn't start out weak. Somehow, this incredibly wise man went off the rails, got sidetracked and bamboozled, and didn't listen to his own advice. Like many of us, he started out strong, confident and committed with unlimited potential and a bright future. Yet he ended up as the classic example of someone getting everything they could ever want and still not being happy.

It didn't begin that way with Solomon, and it usually doesn't begin that way with us.

When Solomon was given the kingdom by his father David, he immediately recognized how inadequate and unprepared he was for the job. So what did he do? He asked the Lord for wisdom.

> **1 Kings 3:7-9** - "Now, O LORD my God, You have made Your servant king instead of my father David, but I am a little child; I do not know how to go out or come in. And Your servant is in the midst of Your people whom You have chosen, a great people, too numerous to be numbered or

counted. Therefore give to Your servant an understanding heart to judge Your people, that I may discern between good and evil. For who is able to judge this great people of Yours?"

Solomon asked for wisdom. The Lord graciously granted his request and gave him more wisdom than anyone has ever had from that time until today. The Lord also gave him what he didn't ask for: riches, honor and a long life (1 Kings 3:11-14). All Solomon had to do was live according to God's wisdom and not by the deceptive human philosophies and carnal teachings of his day (Col. 3:8). Solomon, like many of us, started out strong and then, like the ill-fated Hindenburg, crashed and burned in a spectacular fashion.

Have you ever wondered why?

It was probably because Solomon, like each of us, learned to trust his own instincts and intuition about life and not rely on the "still small voice" of God speaking wisdom into his heart (1 Kings 19:12). Maybe, after a string of earthly successes, Solomon felt he didn't need to rely on God as much now that he viewed himself as a man, rather than a boy. Or maybe Solomon craved the approval of his peers more than the approval of his God. Who knows? Sadly, whatever internal voice led Solomon to his great fall is the same voice we, as individual believers and the church, are listening to today. But be warned. We do this to our own peril and regret.

Our Book of Practical Wisdom

The book of Proverbs, especially the first ten chapters, deals almost exclusively with how to acquire wisdom and why wisdom is so important. Over the next few weeks we will look deeply into God's Book of Wisdom in order to glean all He has to say to us.

My prayer for each of us is that we will heed and follow the wisdom of God and not rely on our own fallen, self-centered, narcissistic, feel-good understanding of the things of God that we know nothing about.

PART ONE

"Wisdom is the right use of knowledge.
To know is not to be wise.
Many men know a great deal, and are all the greater fools for it.
There is no fool so great a fool as a knowing fool.
But to know how to use knowledge is to have wisdom."

— Charles Spurgeon

Get wisdom! Get understanding!
Do not forget, nor turn away from the words of my mouth.
Do not forsake her, and she will preserve you;
Love her, and she will keep you.
Wisdom is the principal thing; therefore get wisdom.
And in all your getting, get understanding.

Proverbs 4:5-7

DAY ONE

More than a Pithy Saying

The proverbs of Solomon the son of David, king of Israel.

Proverbs 1:1

TODAY WE WILL LOOK AT THE WORD *proverb* to discover what it means and why Solomon used this form of teaching to communicate God's wisdom to us.

Solomon wrote over 3,000 proverbs during his lifetime (1 Kings 4:32), yet the Holy Spirit decided to only use the ones found in this book to reveal His unchanging truth to us. It doesn't mean the other sayings of Solomon aren't important. It just means they aren't *inspired*. They're not "God breathed" (2 Tim. 3:16 NIV). They're simply the sayings of a wise man and not the infallible, inerrant words of our sovereign God.[1]

The wise sayings of Solomon aren't the only ones the Lord considered *inspired*. In the book of Proverbs we find sayings from "Agur the son of Jakeh" and someone known as "King Lemuel"

(Prov. 30:1; 31:1), although many Bible scholars think King Lemuel was simply another name for King Solomon.

Suffice it to say, Proverbs is a collection of... well, *proverbs*. They are God-inspired proverbs. Since most of them are from the lips and pen of Solomon, the book is rightly known as the Proverbs of Solomon. But in my opinion, a better title would be: The Proverbs of God, Given to Solomon, to Give to Us.

What is a Proverb?

A *proverb* is defined as a "short, pithy saying in general use stating a truth or piece of advice."[2] Biblically speaking, a *proverb* can be defined as "a short saying that expresses a general truth about God for practical, godly living."[3] For us, the proverbs of Solomon contain the wisdom of God that show us how to live above the sin and degradation of our society and how to understand and fully embrace the "mind of Christ" (1 Cor. 2:16). Proverbs give clear, practical examples on how to "walk in the Spirit" and not "fulfill the lusts of the flesh" (Gal. 5:16). They teach us how to live everyday as an "overcomer" (1 John 5:5) and reveal to us that the "abundant life" Jesus promised is truly obtainable and not something just beyond our grasp (John 10:10). Finally, they present us with a vivid, in-your-face contrast between the painful consequences of choosing the path of the foolish, and the wondrous blessings that come with walking in the way of the wise.

Not all God-inspired proverbs are contained in the book of Proverbs. Other proverbs are found throughout the Old Testament and many are quoted in the New Testament.[4]

Proverbs or "proverbial sayings" are not exclusive to the Scriptures. Every culture has their own set of proverbs, their own

collection of "homespun wisdom" or "short statements of truth."
See if you recognize any of these sayings from American folklore:
"A bird in the hand is worth two in the bush."
"A chain is only as strong as its weakest link."
"A fool and his money are soon parted."
"A friend in need is a friend indeed."
"A penny saved is a penny earned."
"Better safe than sorry."
"Great minds think alike."

In our culture, common-sense sayings like these, often repeated, are considered true.

It is important to recognize the difference between a man-made proverb, which *might* be true, and a God-inspired proverb, which is *always* true. Often the man-made proverb contradicts itself. But that's never the case with the proverbs of Solomon.

Let me give you some examples of this type of inherent contradiction:

"Opposites attract." "Birds of a feather flock together." How can they both be true?

"The early bird gets the worm." "Haste makes waste." Again, these seem like a contradiction to me.

"Clothes make the man." "You cannot judge a book by its cover." If both are true as individual statements, they should also be true when combined. But they're not.

"Absence makes the heart grow fonder." "Out of sight, out of mind." Ouch.

Human proverbs or common, cultural truisms cannot be trusted to be true in *all* situations. They really can't be trusted at all. Proverbs from God, as found in the book of Proverbs, are, like all Scripture, "given by inspiration of God, and profitable for doctrine, for reproof, for correction, for instruction in righteousness" (2 Tim. 3:16). They are God's Word and absolutely true, regardless of man's evolving mindset or changing moral compass.

Why Use Short, Pithy Statements?

Each proverb summarizes a core nugget of a much larger truth, and it does it in a way that's easy to memorize and later recall. For example, John McArthur could preach an hour long, 10,000 plus word sermon on pride and we would be hard pressed to remember much of what he said Monday morning. Solomon, on the other hand, can summarize God's teachings and warnings about pride in just a few, short, easy to remember statements like these:

The promise and warning: "*Pride* goes before destruction, and a haughty spirit before a fall" (Proverbs 16:18).

The warning and the contrast: "When *pride* comes, then comes shame, but with the humble is wisdom" (Proverbs 11:2).

Another warning and contrast: "By *pride* comes nothing but strife, but with the well-advised is wisdom" (Proverbs 13:10).

And finally, the promise and contrast: "A man's *pride* will bring him low, but the humble in spirit will retain honor" (Proverbs 29:23).

God effectively employed, through His servant Solomon, the art of speaking proverbs. The book of Proverbs implants in our heart His power-packed, short statements of truth so that we can easily remember them and "not sin against Him" (Ps. 119:11). Ask yourself which is easier to understand and remember? The 10,000 word sermon with all its examples and rabbit trails, or a concise, eleven word lesson on the consequences of pride?

Proverbs 16:18 - "Pride goes before destruction, and a haughty spirit before a fall."

Give me the eleven words, the catchy song lyric, the short, pithy statement— anytime.

Nothing Left Unturned

As we go through the proverbs of Solomon, remember that each proverb contains a condensed summary, or a bullet point type collection of God's truth found elsewhere in the Scriptures. Proverbs are compact by design, so don't be misled by their size. They're incredibly powerful, like the power that comes from the splitting of a single atom.

God has chosen, for our benefit, to pack as much of Himself as possible into the few words that make up each proverb. If He took the time to specifically choose *each* and *every* word, then we need to spend some time unpacking those words to help us understand the meaning and implication of everything He said.

God never wastes a word in the book of Proverbs. He never wastes anything. He chose the design of the book and the exact words He would use— each consonant, vowel, and syllable— to communicate His wisdom to us.

Getting Serious

1. Have you ever read the entire book of Proverbs? If so, when was that?
2. What was your experience like while reading Proverbs?
3. How long did it take you to complete all thirty-one chapters?
4. Did you then, or are you now, reading more than one chapter a day in Proverbs?
5. Have you ever considered reading one chapter in the book of Proverbs each day for a month?

Next Step Challenge

Would you commit, for the next three weeks, to read the first chapter of Proverbs at least five times each day? Would you also commit to reading it out loud?

Furthermore, would you commit to praying the following prayer each day before reading?

Dear Heavenly Father,

I deeply desire to know You more and to understand You. Would you speak to me today through Your Word and change my life with what You show me?
I pray this in the name of Your Son, Jesus, my Lord. Amen.

Notes

1. In His insightful book *Be Skillful*, Warren Wiersbe gives us the perfect interpretation of 2 Timothy 3:16-17 by saying: "All Scripture is profitable in four ways: (1) for doctrine— that's what's right; (2) for reproof— that's what's not right; (3) for correction— that's how to get right; and (4) for instruction in righteousness— that's how to stay right."

2. The word *pithy* means "something concise or forcefully expressive" and is a word brought back into popular use primarily by Bill O'Riley.

3. Got Questions. "What is a Proverb in the Bible?" accessed March 13, 2016. http://gotquestions.org/proverb-Bible.html.

4. For example, Proverbs 3:11-12 is quoted in Hebrews 12:5-6; Proverbs 3:34 in James 4:6 and 1 Peter 5:5; Proverbs 25:21-22 in Romans 12:20; and Proverbs 26:11 in 2 Peter 2:22. See Wiersbe, W.W. (1996). *Be Skillful*. Wheaton, IL: Victor Books.

DAY TWO

To "Know" What? - Part 1

To know wisdom and instruction,
to perceive the words of understanding.
Proverbs 1:2

O UR CULTURE IS FASCINATED with four-letter words. Believe it or not, the same can be said of the Scriptures. The Word of God places an incredible amount of significance on some simple, four-letter words.

Let me give you a quick example.

Show Me the Love

There are some four-letter words that will transform your entire life once you understand their meaning. "Love" is one of those words. In our culture you can *love* your wife, *love* your children, *love* your job, *love* pizza and ice cream, *love* Fluffy your new pet cat, *love* the way you look in a new pair of jeans, *love* the meal you've just eaten at Cheddars, *love* the Carolina Panthers, and *love* Johnny Depp movies. You can even *love* the deal you got on your new car. In our English definition, all we know is that you have a strong and intense feeling of affection for whatever phrase comes after the word *love*— even if that phrase ranges from your love for your children to your love of ice cream.

In the New Testament, we find several Greek words used to describe different kinds of love. For example, the word *agape* describes the highest form of love, which is the kind of love the Father has for the Son and the Son for the Father (John 5:20). It's the altruistic, self-sacrificing, accepting, benevolent, gracious, all-encompassing and all-giving love that's used in Scripture to communicate the love God has for His creation and for His children.[1]

Next you have *phileo*, which is defined as "brotherly love" or the love between friends. It means to have affection for someone, or to befriend someone.[2] As a side note, God calls us to *agape* our enemies, which means to love them like Christ loves us in order to win them to Him (Matt. 5:44). But He never encourages us to *phileo* our enemies or to befriend them. Why? Because "bad company corrupts good character" every time (1 Cor. 15:33 NIV).

Then you have *eros*, which is the intimate, physical, sexual love a man has for his wife. This is the root of our word *erotic*. It expresses the feelings of arousal shared between people who are physically attracted to each other.[3]

We have three different Greek words, used to describe in great detail, the meaning of a simple, four-letter word. We enjoy and rejoice, for example, in the *agape* of God, yet we would never say we *agape* pizza. We *phileo* our best friend or our college roommate, but would never use *eros* to describe relationships like these. It is important to define and understand even our simple, overused, familiar, four-letter words.

Do You Love Me?

In the last chapter of John we find Jesus restoring His disciples, specifically Peter, in a recorded conversation where Jesus asks Peter, three times, "Do you love Me?" The conversation goes like this:

Jesus: "Simon, son of Jonah, do you love Me more than these?"
Peter: "Yes, Lord; You know that I love You." (John 21:15).
Jesus: "Simon, son of Jonah, do you love Me?"
Peter: "Yes, Lord; You know that I love You." (John 21:16).
Jesus: "Simon, son of Jonah, do you love Me?"
Peter: "Lord, You know all things; You know that I love You." (John 21:17).

The Scriptures say that Peter was grieved because Jesus asked for the third time, "Do you love Me?" (John 21:17). Why was Peter grieved? Was it because Peter didn't think Jesus was paying attention to what he was saying? Was it because Peter didn't like getting grilled in front of his friends? Or maybe Peter wasn't grieved. Maybe he was just annoyed that Jesus kept asking him the same question over and over again and didn't seem to accept his answer.

Unless we understand the meaning of one, simple, four-letter word, we can come up with all sorts of reasons for Peter's grief that are not true. When we study the specific Greek words for love that are used in this conversation, everything becomes crystal clear. There's no longer any reason to guess or assume. Now we know. Here's their conversation in the Greek:

Jesus: "Simon, son of Jonah, do you love (*agape*) Me more than these?"

Peter: "Yes, Lord; You know that I love (*phileo*) You." (John 21:15).

Jesus: "Simon, son of Jonah, do you love (*agape*) Me?"

Peter: "Yes, Lord; You know that I love (*phileo*) You." (John 21:16).

Jesus: "Simon, son of Jonah, do you love (*phileo*) Me?"

Peter: "Lord, You know all things; You know that I love (*phileo*) You." (John 21:17).

Or, to put it in our language:

Jesus: "Peter, do you love (*agape*) Me like I love (*agape*) you? Do you love (*agape*) Me with an unselfish and self-sacrificing love (*agape*) like I love (*agape*) you?"

Peter: "Lord, I love (*phileo*) You like a friend."

Jesus: "Peter, do you love (*agape*) Me like I love (*agape*) You? Do you love (*agape*) Me with the highest form of love (*agape*)?"

Peter: "Lord, I love (*phileo*) You like a friend, like my best friend."

Jesus: "Peter, do you really just love (*phileo*) Me like a friend?"

Peter: "Lord, You know all things; You know that I love (*phileo*) You like my friend, like a pal, my best buddy and my BFF."

It is now apparent why Peter was grieved the third time Jesus spoke. The true meaning of a small, four-letter word can change our entire understanding of what the Scriptures truly say.

Yada and Ginosko

This brings us to another vital, four-letter word. The word is *know*. To *know* how. To *know* what. To *know* something. To be in the *know*. To have *know*ledge. To ac*know*ledge someone.

There are several Greek and Hebrew words used to describe and define a clear and concise picture of what the single word *know* actually means. Until we unpack these words, we'll never understand the glorious depth of what the Lord is revealing to us in His Word. We'll get lazy and let our English definition of what we think the word means cloud the truth He is telling us today.

In Proverbs 1:2 we read that one of the purposes of this great book is: "To *know* wisdom and instruction, to perceive the words of understanding."

But what does the word, *know* (*yada* in Hebrew and *ginosko* in the Greek) really mean?

Next we'll look at this powerful four-letter word and see exactly how the Lord uses it to give us a lasting understanding of what it means to "*know* wisdom and instruction" (Prov. 1:2) and also what it means when Jesus says, "I am the good shepherd; and I *know* My sheep, and am *known* by My own" (John 10:14).

15

Getting Serious

1. What does the word *love* mean to you?
2. Can you use *agape*, *phileo* and *eros* to describe the different kinds of love in your life?
3. Will you, from now on, circle the word *love* each time you read a passage and indicate for yourself which Greek word is used?
4. What do you think it means to "know wisdom"? How would you define wisdom?
5. Can you describe a time when you felt God had given you His wisdom? What was that like? If you have never had that experience, why not? Can you think of a reason why God hasn't given you His wisdom in a particular situation? Do you want that to change?

Next Step Challenge

Grab a Word Study, like Vines or Zodhiates, or go to www.blueletterbible.com and do a simple, online word search for "know" in both the Old and New Testament. Notice the different ways the word is translated in the English. What do these differences say to you?

Then examine John 21:17 (see below) and notice the two different words translated "know" in this passage. What is the Lord trying to tell us?

> He said to him the third time, "Simon, son of Jonah, do you love Me?" Peter was grieved because He said to him the third time, "Do you

love Me?" And he said to Him, "Lord, You know (*eido*) all things; You know (*ginosko*) that I love You." Jesus said to him, "Feed My sheep."

Finally, look up the meaning of *eido* (1492 in Strong's)[4] and *ginosko* (1097 in Strong's) and write this verse again using the proper meaning of the Greek words for *love* and for *know*.

Does this statement by the Lord seem clearer to you?

Notes

1. Zodhiates, S. (2000). The complete word study dictionary: New Testament. (pp. 64-66). Chattanooga, TN: AMG Publishers.
2. Ibid., 1445.
3. Got Questions. "What is Eros Love?" accessed on March 21, 2016. http://gotquestions.org/eros-love.html.
4. When I use the reference *Strong's*, I am referring to the notation in the Strong's Concordance where every Hebrew and Greek word is given a numerical value. Therefore, you don't necessarily have to know Greek or Hebrew, but can simply match the Strong's number with the word in Scripture to discover its use and definition. For example, love (*agape*) is Strong's #25, and love (*phileo*) is Strong's #5368. You can find a Strong's Concordance in any Christian bookstore, or online at sites like www.blueletterbible.com and www.biblestudytools.com.

DAY THREE

To "Know" What? - Part 2

To know wisdom and instruction,
to perceive the words of understanding.
Proverbs 1:2

THE LORD TELLS US IN HIS PREAMBLE of
Proverbs that one of the purposes of this great book is for us
"to *know* wisdom and instruction" and "to perceive the words of
understanding" (Prov. 1:2). Then, BAM! There it is again, right
before our eyes— another troubling four letter word.

This time the word isn't love, but *know*. What does it mean to
know something, such as wisdom and instruction? What does it
mean to be in the *know*, to have *know*ledge, or to ac*know*ledge
someone or something?

Our contemporary definition of *know* is "to be aware of
something through careful observation, inquiry, or information; to

19

develop a relationship with someone through meeting and spending time with them, to be familiar or friendly."[1]

"Oh, ask me. I *know* the answer to that question."
"You don't have to remind me. I *know* I have to pick them up at the airport at 5:00pm."
"I *know* who you are. I recognized you from your Facebook profile."
"I *know* all about Abraham Lincoln. I read about him in my textbook."

There are several different words that are translated *know* in the Scriptures: In the Greek, primarily *eido* (1492 in Strong's) and *ginosko* (1097 in Strong's), and in the Hebrew, *yada* (3045 in Strong's). The Hebrew word *yada* is essentially the same as the Greek word *ginosko*. So let's take a few minutes and dig a bit deeper into the difference between knowing something (*eido*) versus knowing someone (*ginosko* or *yada*) and why that's even important.

Do You Know with Your Head or Your Heart?

This is the question that defines these two words and describes the different aspects of what it means to *know*. Is it merely head knowledge, meaning the accumulation of facts and raw data? Or can I *know* someone on a more personal level, with more intimacy and passion? Can I *know* them by my experience with them and not just *know* facts about them?

In the Greek, *eido* (1492) is defined as "to see, to perceive with the eyes or the senses, to observe, to get or gain knowledge of something, to understand."[2] It's a mental, cognitive retention of some facts. It's head knowledge, or book learning. It's preparing for your final exam by memorizing all the answers and then forgetting them immediately after the test is over. It's knowing, for example, that George Washington was the first president of the United States, yet that fact having absolutely no impact on your daily life.

There's another word translated *know* that means something altogether different. The word *ginosko* (1097) means "to know in a completed sense, to know everything and to know in full, to learn to know; it also means to know by intimate experience or expression; to choose, to approve, to love, to embrace, to desire, to place one's favor upon."[3]

One can *know* something by studying the facts (*eido*) or one can *know* by choosing to live the experience (*ginosko*) and loving every minute of it. The first meaning is dry, academic and sterile (*eido*). The second is complete, life-changing and exhilarating (*ginosko*).

Let me give you a few examples.

"And (Joseph) did not *know* her (*ginosko* - to know by intimate experience or expression, to choose, to love, to desire, to place one's favor upon) till she had brought forth her firstborn Son. And he called His name Jesus"(Matt. 1:25). This word, in both the Old and New Testament, is used as a euphemism for sexual relations between two people. "Now Adam *knew* (*yada*) Eve his wife, and she conceived and bore Cain" (Gen. 4:1). When Adam *knew* Eve it was obviously more than just memorizing a few facts about her.

But Jesus said, "Somebody touched Me, for I *perceived* (*ginosko* - to know by intimate experience or expression) power going out from Me" (Luke 8:46). Jesus *knew* (*ginosko*), not by reading a book or sitting in a classroom (*eido*), that something had happened to

21

Him. He personally experienced power going out from Him to the woman with the issue of blood. He *knew* (*ginosko*), without being told, that power had gone out from Him because He experienced it Himself.

I Know My Sheep

There are incredible passages that show the choice, desire, love, approval and favor associated with Jesus *knowing* (*ginosko*) those who belong to Him. These passages do not reference cognitive head knowledge. They refer to something deeper and much more intimate. Jesus is knowing, choosing, loving, approving and desiring those He places His favor upon— those called the elect in Him (Rom. 8:33).

"I am the good shepherd; and I *know* (*ginosko*) My sheep, and am *known* (*ginosko*) by My own" (John 10:14). Jesus *knows* (*ginosko*) those who belong to Him. He *knows* (*ginosko*) them intimately. He has chosen them, approved of them, embraced them, and has placed His favor upon them. The elect— those He has chosen for His own— also *know* (*ginosko*) Him in return. They don't just *know* (*eido*) about Jesus. They *know* (*ginosko*) Jesus by intimate experience and expression. They also choose Him, desire Him, love Him and belong to Him.

It's important to note that Jesus *knows* (*eido*) everything and everyone because He is a sovereign God. But He only *knows* (*ginosko*) those who are His own, those who belong to Him, those He has chosen— His sheep.

It gets even better.

"As the Father *knows* (*ginosko*) Me, even so I *know* (*ginosko*) the Father; and I lay down My life for the sheep" (John 10:15). As the Father completely and fully, with intimate experience and expression, *knows* (*ginosko*) the Son, so the Son— the second Person of the Trinity— also *knows* (*ginosko*) the Father in the same way.

I Never Knew You

"And then I will declare to them, 'I never *knew* (*ginosko*) you; depart from Me, you who practice lawlessness!'" (Matt. 7:23). This certainly doesn't mean there was a body of knowledge in the universe or a group of people the Son of God was unaware of. It doesn't mean there was something He had to learn, something that slipped His mind, a skill He had yet to master, or something He forgot. "Uh, I'm sorry. What was your name again?" No, Jesus *knows* (*eido*) all. He is God, and among other things, He is omniscient.

This use of *ginosko* means there are some whom He has not chosen; some He doesn't have an intimate, loving experience with; some whom He has not placed His favor upon and some He does not desire or approve of. Who are these people? Jesus answered, "You who practice lawlessness!" (Matt. 7:23). You who reject His love, mercy and sacrifice. You who are lost, unredeemed and unrepentant of your sins.

To Know Wisdom and Instruction

In summary, when you come across the word *know* in the Scriptures, please understand it can have a far deeper meaning than just being aware of something after careful observation or memorization of certain facts that pertain to it. The word you read can mean to *know* (*eido*) in a general, mental, cognitive way or it can mean something much deeper (*ginosko*) that involves experience, intimacy, volition and love.

It's also important to understand that *ginosko* in the Greek is essentially the same word as *yada* in the Hebrew. When we read in the book of Proverbs: "To *know* (*yada*) wisdom and instruction, to perceive the words of understanding," it means we are to *know* (*yada*) in a completed sense; to know everything and to know fully; to learn to know. It means to know by intimate experience or expression; to choose, to approve, to love, to embrace, to desire, to place one's favor upon.

What are we to *know* (*yada*)? Wisdom and instruction. What do wisdom and instruction mean? How can we choose to have an intimate experience with both? How can we know (*yada*) them completely and fully as the Scriptures command?

Stay tuned, because that's exactly what we'll be examining next.

Getting Serious

1. When you read the word *know*, do you mentally define it as *eido* or *ginosko*? Which one do you naturally default to?
2. What resource do you use to discover the deeper meaning of the Greek and Hebrew words in your Bible?
3. How long have you been using that resource? What do you like about it and what are its shortcomings?
4. Is taking more time to study your Bible difficult for you? If so, do you know why? Do you put the same effort into studying God's Word as you would, for example, a college history exam? If not, do you know why?
5. On a scale from 1 to 10, how would you rate your desire for God's Word at this point in your life? What was it three months ago? One year ago? Are you growing in your faith or standing still? Finally, what are you prepared to do about it?

Next Step Challenge

During your personal Bible reading time, commit to making it a practice of looking up each instance of the word *know* and marking in your Bible if it's *ginosko* or *eido*, or maybe another Greek word. You might even choose to write above them the Strong's reference number: 1097 for *ginosko* and 1492 for *eido*.

Then look to discover any other words that translate *ginosko* (such as comprehend, learn, realize, notice, understand, etc.) or *eido* (such as see, behold, perceive, etc.) to help you further understand the meaning of the Scripture you study.

Finally, make a list of the verses in order to get a better understanding of how these words are translated in various passages of Scriptures.

Are you beginning to see the depths of God's Word and the importance even small words can bring to your understanding of the Scriptures? Do you find your hunger for more of Him growing? If so, how are you going to satisfy that hunger? What are your plans? And if your hunger for more of Him is not growing, do you know why?

Whatever your answers are to these questions, what are you prepared to do about it?

Notes

1. *Know.* (1989) In Oxford English Dictionary online (2nd ed.). Retrieved from http://dictionary.com.
2. Zodhiates, S. (2000). The complete word study dictionary: New Testament. (pp. 508-510). Chattanooga, TN: AMG Publishers.
3. Ibid., 372-373.

DAY FOUR

How to Become a "Wise Guy"

To know wisdom and instruction,
to perceive the words of understanding.
Proverbs 1:2

IN PROVERBS 1:2 WE DISCOVERED that one of the
great goals of the book of Proverbs is to allow us to *know*, in an
intimate and experiential sense, both wisdom and instruction.
We've already looked at what the word *know* means in this
passage. But what about *wisdom* and *instruction?*

Wisdom is defined as "the quality of having experience,
knowledge, and good judgment, or the quality of being wise. It's
the ability to discern or judge what is right, true and lasting."[1]
Wisdom is not the mere accumulation of facts about someone or
something. It is the ability to properly *apply* those facts in a given
situation to determine the right and God-honoring outcome.
Wisdom is manifested when a person can see the circumstances

they face, match them with truth they know from God's Word, and then plot a correct course of action that is based on biblical truth, rather than the urgency of the situation.

Instruction is not primarily defined as teaching or exhortation, as we would expect. Instruction (*musar*) is defined as "discipline, chastening, and correction, with the imagery of a father disciplining his son."[2] The book of Proverbs is designed to help us know (*yada*) by doing; to learn by experience in an intimate, personal way; to discern what is right, true, and lasting (versus choosing the cheap trinkets and toys our culture offers). We are to learn the wisdom of God by discipline, correction and chastening because "whom the Lord loves He chastens" (Heb. 12:6).

How Do We Get Wisdom?

There are several verses that speak to this desire. The most well-known is found in James:

> **James 1:5-8** - If any of you lacks wisdom, let him ask of God, who gives to all liberally and without reproach, and it will be given to him. But let him ask in faith, with no doubting, for he who doubts is like a wave of the sea driven and tossed by the wind. For let not that man suppose that he will receive anything from the Lord; he is a double-minded man, unstable in all his ways.

As seen in this passage, wisdom is given to anyone who asks, as long as they ask in faith. If they doubt when they ask, they should not expect to receive anything from the Lord. Why? Because they are "double-minded" and "unstable" in all their ways (James 1:8).

Let's get this straight. If we take this passage at face value then all we have to do is ask for the wisdom of God and He will lavishly give His wisdom to us, or to anyone for that matter, just as long as we ask in faith, without doubting. There are no additional requirements. No standards that must be met. No waiting lines or limited quantities. We just ask in faith and God gives us His wisdom.

But what does God's wisdom look like? Is it something that God possesses within Himself, as a part of Himself, like an extension of His divine nature? Is it a character trait He has and then freely shares with those who ask?

If getting God's wisdom is so easy, then what's the point of the book of Proverbs? If all we have to do is pray in order to receive God's wisdom, why do we need the Bible as our instruction manual? Can we really become as wise as Solomon by just asking?

Or is there something or Someone we're missing?

Wisdom is Found in Just One Man

If we keep looking for the true meaning of wisdom in His Word, we will soon find ourselves walking through the pages of 1 Corinthians where we find:

> **1 Corinthians 1:30** - But of Him you are in Christ Jesus, who became for us *wisdom* from God— and righteousness and sanctification and redemption.

Jesus, by His own doing, has literally become for us the "wisdom from God." When we see Jesus, we see all the "wisdom from God" in perfect clarity. If we want to know (*yada*) the "wisdom from God" we need to know (*yada*) the Son of God. Since Jesus has "become for us wisdom from God" we need only to look and learn from Him to have wondrous wisdom. If we want more wisdom, we must seek and ask for more of Jesus.

The answer for our lack of wisdom is Jesus. It's all about Jesus.

James speaks of asking God for wisdom and knowing that God gives "liberally and without reproach" to all who ask (James 1:5). James might be speaking of the wisdom found only in Jesus. Or, he might just be speaking about Jesus Himself.

Consider the passage again:

> **James 1:5** - If any of you lacks *wisdom* (what Jesus literally became for us - 1 Cor. 1:30), let him ask God (for more of Jesus, for the revelation of Jesus, to receive Jesus) who gives (Jesus) to all ("Come unto Me, *all* you who labor and are heavy laden" - Matt. 11:28) liberally and without reproach (there is therefore now no condemnation to those who are in Christ Jesus - Rom. 8:1), and it will be given to him (to make us complete in Christ - Col. 2:10).

To Know Wisdom is to Know Jesus

It is Jesus who has become for us "wisdom from God — and righteousness, and sanctification and redemption" (1 Cor. 1:30). It is only Jesus, and none other.

Proverbs 1 clarifies the main purpose of the entire book. The purpose is for us to know (*yada*) wisdom. But that wisdom also refers to *knowing* Jesus, the life in Christ, and how to live in Him in a practical, hands-on, everyday sense. Proverbs gives us instruction on godly living and examples of how to put into practice the wisdom found in Christ. He's our perfect example, who "was in all points tempted as we are, yet without sin" (Heb. 4:15).

When we want to know how to respond to someone who verbally attacks our loved ones, we can look to Jesus, the "author and finisher of our faith" (Heb. 12:2), and see how He responded in the same situation. We see His perfect example and, like true disciples, follow Him who has become for us the "wisdom from God" (1 Cor. 1:30). When our rights are violated and we scream for justice or vengeance, what should we do? We look to Jesus and do what He did. We learn from Him. We learn His wisdom by learning more about Him, walking with Him, and choosing to live like Him.

This is what it means to know (*yada*) wisdom and instruction. It means to know (*yada*) Jesus (wisdom) and to be disciplined, instructed disciples of His. The answer to our lack of wisdom is always our lack of Jesus.

The book of Proverbs gives us hands on examples of how Jesus would handle a situation that wasn't recorded in the Bible. For example, how would Jesus handle sexual temptation? Or how would He deal with peer pressure?

In the next chapter we'll see how the book of Proverbs completes the life of Christ not recorded in the gospels of Matthew, Mark, Luke and John.

Getting Serious

1. What does it mean for you, in a practical sense, to see Jesus as the wisdom from God (Col. 1:30)?
2. Do you have the wisdom of God? How do you know, one way or the other?
3. Since *instruction* in our passage primarily means discipline, how disciplined are you in your walk with Christ? Do you have daily time with Him? When, where, and for how long?
4. Can you remember an example of God giving you His wisdom at just the right time? What was the experience like? How often does it happen to you?
5. On a scale from 1 to 10, how would you rate God's wisdom in your life and in your decision making process? What was it three months ago? How about one year ago? Are you growing in His wisdom or are you stagnated?

Next Step Challenge

Use a Bible Concordance, or an online source like www.blueletterbible.com, to do a search of the word "wisdom" in both the Old and the New Testament. Write down at least twenty passages that speak to you personally. Do you see any differences in the description of wisdom in the Old Testament compared to the New Testament? If so, what are those differences?

On a separate sheet of paper, write down the twenty passages you chose.

Why did you choose the twenty passages that you did?

What has the Lord shown you through your word search and those twenty passages?

Notes

1. Baker, W., & Carpenter, E. E. (2003). The complete word study dictionary: Old Testament (p. 337). Chattanooga, TN: AMG Publishers.
2. Ibid., 582.

DAY FIVE

Jesus is Our Wisdom

To know wisdom and instruction,
to perceive the words of understanding.
Proverbs 1:2

WE DISCOVERED YESTERDAY, in 1 Corinthians 1:30, that Jesus "became for us wisdom from God— and righteousness and sanctification and redemption." This verse clearly shows that Jesus Christ is, within Himself, the wisdom from God. Jesus is all wisdom, totally complete in Himself. If we desire more wisdom from the Father (James 1:5), He answers by revealing more of His Son. We *ask* for wisdom. We get Jesus. We *look* for wisdom. We see it in Jesus. If we want to *know* wisdom (Prov. 1:2), we must *know* none other but Jesus.

The wisdom from God is found in only one person.

His name is Jesus.

To Know and Perceive

Proverbs begins by telling us that the grand purpose of the book is "to know (*yada*) wisdom and instruction, (and) to perceive the words of understanding" (Prov. 1:2).

Wisdom, as we know, is "the ability to discern or judge what is right, true, and lasting."[1] Instruction involves more than teaching or exhortation. *Instruction* is "discipline, chastening, and correction, with the imagery of a father disciplining his son that he loves."[2]

To *perceive* means "to discern, consider, understand, to be attentive or pay attention to."[3] Further, *words of understanding* mean "words or speech of comprehension, discernment, righteous actions, with a strong moral and religious connotation."[4] In other words, "to perceive the words of understanding" is not something to be mentally perceived or discerned. Rather, it's to follow through on what we perceive with righteous actions, works, or deeds that have a strong moral and religious connotation. This brings about God's wisdom and the ability to choose what is right, true and lasting.

The purpose of Proverbs is for us to know (*yada*) by experience, or by doing, in an intimate, passionate way, the wisdom of God— through Jesus Christ (1 Cor. 1:30), and possess the ability to discern and choose what is right and godly in any given circumstance. The New Testament calls this sanctification (1 Thess. 4:3), having the "mind of Christ" (1 Cor. 2:16), or walking in the Spirit, and not according to the flesh (Gal. 5:16).

Its purpose is for us to know wisdom— the wisdom found only in Christ (1 Cor. 1:30), and to be "complete in Him" (Col. 2:10).

Our Only Example During Temptation and Sin

In Hebrews, there's another verse that gives us a deeper, clearer understanding of why Jesus "became for us wisdom from God" (1 Cor. 1:30). It's found in Hebrews 4:15:

> **Hebrews 4:15** - For we do not have a High Priest (Jesus) who cannot *sympathize* (feel deeply, be affected or touched with the same feelings as another, to have compassion for someone by experience)[5] with our *weaknesses* (feebleness, lack of strength, frailty),[6] but was in *all points* (each, every, the whole, in totality, lacking none)[7] *tempted* (tried, tested)[8] as we are, yet without sin.

This tells us that Jesus, our wisdom from God, was tempted in every way we have been tempted, yet was able and willing to discern what was right, best and true, and was then disciplined enough to choose the right path and not sin. He was tested in all ways like each one of us. Therefore, He is our faithful High Priest that goes before us "perceiving the words of understanding" (Prov. 1:2) and showing us, by example, how to live victoriously by knowing (*yada*) and following the wisdom of God.

Let's go a little deeper.

Was Jesus ever tempted by pride? Are you? Then so was He. Every temptation you have faced, or will face, He's already faced and walked in perfect holiness and unity with His Father. We are to follow His example.

Was Jesus ever tempted sexually? Have you been tempted that way? Then so was He, yet without giving into sin. If you feel overpowered by porn or sexual temptation, know that Jesus faced the same temptation and resisted, so as not to sin. If we keep our eyes on Him and follow His example, we can victoriously walk away from every temptation, just as Jesus did.

New Testament Examples

Jesus lived His life in perfect harmony with the Father, just like He desires us to do. We can follow His example by taking His yoke upon us and learning from Him (Matt. 11:29). In the pages of Matthew, Mark, Luke and John, Jesus gave us example after example of how to "know wisdom and instruction (and how) to perceive the words of understanding" (Prov. 1:2). If we're faced with a situation that Jesus also faced, we can go to the account of how He dealt with it and learn from Him. As faithful disciples, we mimic our Master.

For example, how do we handle it when someone abuses us and demands something they don't rightly deserve? What did Jesus do? He turned the other cheek (Luke 6:29) and walked the second mile (Matt. 5:41). What are we to do when we feel betrayed by someone we trusted and are tempted to harbor hate and bitterness toward them in our heart? What did Jesus do? In the upper room, Jesus washed the feet of Judas (John 13:5).

But what happens when we're faced with a temptation not recorded in the gospel accounts? We know Jesus was tempted in all ways, just like we are (Heb. 4:15), yet not everything Jesus said or did is recorded for us in the gospels (John 21:25). We know almost nothing about His life as a young man, for example. So where do we go to learn what Jesus, our wisdom from God, would do in a particular situation we encounter today that is not mentioned in the Scriptures?

We go to the book of Proverbs.

Proverbs give us the wisdom from God (what Jesus would do) in situations and circumstances not mentioned in the gospels. Proverbs fill in for us what the gospels left out.

Consider the following examples:

Peer Pressure: Do you face the temptation to compromise in order to be accepted by your peers? If so, you can be sure Jesus faced the same temptation. Yet, how He dealt with this temptation is not recorded for us in the gospel accounts. So where do we go to find what Jesus did and what we should do when faced with peer pressure? We go to the book of Proverbs. If you struggle with peer pressure and want to know what Jesus did when He was faced with peer pressure, go to Proverbs 1:8-19.

How about:

Sexual Temptation: See Proverbs 5:1-11.
Pride: Proverbs 11:2, 13:10, 16:18, 29:23.
Financial Obligations: Proverbs 6:1-5.
Adultery: Proverbs 6:20-35.
Porn: Proverbs 7:6-23.
Business Practices: Proverbs 11:1.
What to Look for in a Wife: Proverbs 31:10-31.

The list could go on and on.

When you hold the book of Proverbs in your hand to read, don't view it as the ancient writings of an old sage who can't relate to what you're going through. Scriptural proverbs are the words, examples and wisdom of Christ. They're His example to us of how He, as the wisdom from God, was able to live victoriously in this world of sin, without sinning. They're His answer to our temptations not specifically addressed in the gospel accounts. They're His incredible gift to each of us.

Embrace them, cherish them, love them, and know (*yada*) them as your way "to know wisdom and instruction, (and) to perceive the words of understanding" (Prov. 1:2).

After all, Jesus did say:

> **John 5:39** - "You search the Scriptures, for in them you think you have eternal life; and these are they which testify of Me."

All Scripture, in both the Old and New Testament, speaks or testifies of Jesus Christ, including the book of Proverbs.

Getting Serious

1. Does it seem strange to think Jesus was tempted in the same way you are tempted?

2. Do you view Jesus as some super-human who lived above the cesspool you and I find ourselves in? Do you think that Jesus was never tempted in the same way you are?

3. Did it ever occur to you that the entire Scriptures, both Old and New Testament, testify about Jesus? Did you ever consider the fact that He can be found on every page, in almost every verse?

4. When was the last time God spoke to you through His Word? What was the experience like? How often does it happen to you?

5. On a scale from 1 to 10, how would you rate God's wisdom in your life right now and in your decision making process? What was it yesterday? Are you growing in the wisdom of God? If not, why not?

Next Step Challenge

Using your Bible and the examples in this chapter, outline the specific situations addressed in Proverbs. List them on a sheet of paper along with the Scripture reference. What do they tell you about Jesus and His Word? What have you learned about the true purpose and meaning of the book of Proverbs?

How will you let what you've learned change your life from this point forward?

Notes

1. Baker, W., & Carpenter, E. E. (2003). The complete word study dictionary: Old Testament (p. 337). Chattanooga, TN: AMG Publishers.
2. Ibid., 582.
3. Ibid., 129-130.
4. Ibid., 130.
5. Zodhiates, S. (2000). The complete word study dictionary: New Testament. (p. 1328). Chattanooga, TN: AMG Publishers.
6. Ibid., 270-273.
7. Ibid., 1125-1127.
8. Ibid., 1135-1136.

DAY SIX

Wisdom is a Choice,
So Choose Wisely

To know wisdom and instruction,
to perceive the words of understanding,
to receive the instruction of wisdom,
justice, judgment, and equity.
Proverbs 1:2-3

THE QUESTION OFTEN ASKED is how did Solomon actually receive the wisdom of God? How did it come about? What was his experience like? What was the process?

From the account in 1 Kings, we find little to shed light on the specific details of that momentous event. We *do* find that Solomon was overwhelmed with the responsibility of leading the kingdom he inherited from his father David. He recognized that he was but "a little child" who didn't "know how to go out or come in" (1 Kings 3:7). Then, in a marvelous way, God granted his request and gave him not only a "wise and understanding heart" (1 Kings 3:12), but also threw in what Solomon didn't ask for: "both riches and honor" (1 Kings 3:13). Why? Simply because He wanted to and because He could.

From then on, we see Solomon sometimes acting in the wisdom God gave him and, at other times, living like a rich, spoiled brat who made "dumb as a brick" decisions for himself, his family, and the nation God trusted him to lead.

How is that possible? How could a man who was given the very wisdom of God make such dumb, lousy, selfish decisions? Didn't God make Solomon a wise man when He gave him His wisdom?

When God gives someone His wisdom, does that mean *everything* they say or do is wise and from God from that point forward?

Solomon Was Not a Wise Man

Let's nip this one in the bud right out of the gate. Solomon was *not* an inherently wise man. He was *not* one whose very nature oozed wisdom. How could he be? The decisions and choices he made as a father, husband and king were anything but wise and sadly reflected his true nature. When Solomon relied on the wisdom of God, he made incredibly wise decisions— some that we still marvel at today. When left to himself, Solomon made decisions and choices according to his own nature, based on what he was made of on the inside. Indeed, Solomon's nature was anything but wise.

The same is true of you and me.

It was certainly not wise for a husband to have 700 wives and 300 concubines (1 Kings 11:3). Think of the infighting within his own family. Imagine how used and rejected his wives felt, not to mention the concubines. Solomon's selfish, unwise decision to marry so many women wasn't a momentary lapse of reason. It wasn't something he did and regretted later, vowing to never make the same mistake again. This pattern of thinking was habitual, ingrained, and occurred at least another 999 times.

Among his children, hatred, jealousy, bigotry and bitterness was the rule of the day. What does this tell us about Solomon's nature and core values regarding his fatherly responsibilities? Where's the wisdom in any of this?

Finally, Solomon's spiritual leadership was practically non-existent. He allowed his many wives to desecrate the sanctity of his own home, the holiness of the Temple of God, and the entire nation. His wives built altars to their foreign gods and brought idolatry into the land. How could Solomon allow this to take place under his watch? How could one man be so wise and yet fail so miserably? Solomon's true nature revealed the carnality, apathy, and weakness of Solomon the man, in contrast to the inherent wisdom often attributed to him.

Wisdom is a Choice

The wisdom Solomon received from the Lord is the same thing you and I receive in Christ. Solomon received wisdom, while you and I receive Christ into our lives, "who became for us wisdom from God" (1 Cor. 1:30). Once we've received Christ, it's up to us to live and "walk in the Spirit, and not fulfill the lust of the flesh" (Gal. 5:16). As with Solomon, it becomes a choice— a simple, but difficult choice.

When we choose to live according to the new nature within us, based on the wisdom given to us by Christ and administered by the Holy Spirit, we will naturally make wise decisions. This is because we "walk in the Spirit" (Gal. 5:16) and have the "mind of Christ" (1 Cor. 2:16). When we choose to go our own way, to call the shots as we see fit, or to live according to the flesh, we can expect our end to be the same as Solomon's. It is the exercise of our own free will to choose either the blessings of a life of submission to Christ or the heartache of a life brought on by the rebellion of our flesh.

Once you've chosen wisely, your job's not done. You still have to act on that choice.

Look at the transition about wisdom in Proverbs 1:2-3.

> To *know* wisdom and instruction, to perceive the words of understanding,
> To *receive* the instruction of wisdom, justice, judgment, and equity.

First we are to "know" wisdom in Proverbs 1:2 and then "receive" the instruction of wisdom in the next verse. We go from *knowing* to *receiving* in the space of twenty words. One is an understanding of something and the other is a choice. It is an action based on that choice— the *receiving* of something found only in Him.

We can "know" wisdom (Jesus Christ), truth, right from wrong, good and evil, up from down, and all sorts of wonderful things, and yet still choose to live contrary to what we "know". Unfortunately, like Solomon, we will suffer the terrible consequences of our bad choices. Or we can *know* the truth and *choose* the truth and be *set free* by the truth (John 8:32).

Easy? No. Simple? Absolutely.

Wisdom is a Gift

In other words, the wisdom Solomon received from the Lord is the same wisdom available to each of us today through the residing presence of the Holy Spirit. We already have *in* us and available *to* us the same wisdom of God that was given to Solomon. How? By virtue of being "in Christ Jesus who became for us wisdom from God" (1 Cor. 1:30). The key to living in the gift of wisdom boils down to what we do with the gift. Do we "receive (or choose to receive) the instruction (discipline, correction, chastisement) of wisdom" (Prov. 1:3), or do we hide it away and let it die from inactivity and lack of use? Jesus said that we are the "light of the world". He commands us to place the light of our lives (which includes His wisdom, redeeming power, and grace in us) like a lamp on the table for the whole world to see (Matt. 5:14-16).

It's more than just "knowing." It's "receiving" and having the discipline (instruction) to obey what we've received.

It Comes in One Package

Consider the passage in Galatians where it says the "works (plural) of the flesh are evident" (Gal. 5:19-21). The "works" are then listed, one by one: adultery, fornication, uncleanness, lewdness, idolatry, sorcery, hatred and the like. These "works" or "deeds" of the flesh are freestanding, independent, and not part of a combined package. You can have one or more of these but not necessarily all. For example, you can commit adultery, but not murder. You can have hatred and selfish ambition, but not participate in idolatry or sorcery. The word "works" or "deeds" is plural. This means that many individual works (not just one work) are made up of many individual parts.

The "fruit" of the Spirit is just the opposite. It's singular. *One* fruit is made up of a combination of nine different attributes: love (agape), joy, peace, longsuffering, kindness, goodness, faithfulness, gentleness and self-control (Gal. 5:22-23). If you have one, you have them all. They come in a package. It's all or nothing.

This is how we receive wisdom from the Lord.

We receive wisdom through Jesus (the one fruit) and all the attributes (the fullness of the Godhead) that dwell in Him bodily. Being "in Christ", we are complete in Him (Col. 2:9-10).

You and I have the same Spirit. Thus we have the same wisdom available to us that was given to Solomon. All we have to do is rely on that wisdom, which is the residing presence of the Holy Spirit, for God's wisdom to manifest itself in us.

How is Our Experience Different from Solomon's?

The same thing that happened to Solomon happened to each of us when we received Christ as Lord and the Holy Spirit came to make us His home, or to abide in us. When He came, so did His wisdom. It's always there, always available and always ready. Solomon received what we received, but only in part. He received wisdom from God. We, on the other hand, received God Himself (Christ), who became for us the "wisdom from God" (1 Cor. 1:30)— and so much more.

We need, maybe even more than Solomon, to rest in God's wisdom and "walk (think, live, and choose) in (according to) the Spirit." For this is how we shall not fulfill, like Solomon, the "lust of the flesh" (Gal. 5:16).

Let's get started living in the inheritance and wisdom God has already provided us as "joint heirs with Christ" (Rom. 8:17).

Getting Serious

1. Did you ever wonder how Solomon was given the wisdom from God? Did you ever want to know how that same wisdom could be given to you?
2. Did you ever think the wisdom given to Solomon was something only given to special saints and not to ordinary, everyday people like you and me? If so, why did you think that?
3. How does it make you feel to know, or at least to entertain the thought, that you already possess the wisdom Solomon had by virtue of the Holy Spirit living in you? In fact, by being "in Christ" you possess much more than Solomon. How does that make you feel?
4. Let me ask this again: When was the last time God spoke to you through His Word? What was that experience like? How often does it happen?
5. On a scale from 1 to 10, how would you rate God's wisdom in your life right now and in your decision making process? What was it yesterday? Are you growing in the wisdom of God? If not, why not?

Next Step Challenge

Use your Bible and look up at least twenty-five passages where the term "in Christ" is found. What do they say about your life right now? For starters, you can begin with four verses from Romans, provided below.

Romans 6:11 - Likewise you also, reckon yourselves to be dead indeed to sin, but alive to God (how) *in Christ* Jesus our Lord.

Romans 6:23 - For the wages of sin is death, but the gift of God is eternal life (how) *in Christ* Jesus our Lord.

Romans 8:1 - There is therefore now no condemnation to those who are (what) *in Christ* Jesus, who do not walk according to the flesh, but according to the Spirit.

Romans 12:5 - So we, being many, are one body (how) *in Christ*, and individually members of one another.

How will you let what you've learned change your life from this point forward?

DAY SEVEN

Four Verbs— Part One

To know wisdom and instruction,
to perceive the words of understanding,
to receive the instruction of wisdom, justice, judgment,
and equity; to give prudence to the simple,
to the young man knowledge and discretion.
Proverbs 1:2-4

AS WE DIG DEEPER INTO THE book of Proverbs we quickly come across a few arresting verbs: *know, perceive, receive,* and *give.* We also see the corresponding nouns associated with each of these verbs. In Proverbs 1:2-4 we find:

> To *know* wisdom and instruction,
> To *perceive* the words of understanding,
> To *receive* the instruction of wisdom, justice, judgment, and equity;

To *give* prudence to the simple (and give) to the young man knowledge and discretion.

Notice the natural progression of action. First, to *know*. Second, to *perceive* something. Third, to choose to personally *receive* and embrace what we now know and perceive. And finally, to share— to *give* what we have now received to someone else.

But what does it mean to *perceive* a new truth or a deeper understanding of a known truth? How does someone *receive* a truth or understanding to themselves that they have just perceived? What does the process look like, and how does the exchange actually happen? Ultimately, to whom do we *give* what we have received, and what specifically do we give them?

The answer is found in the nouns connected with our actions.

Let's begin by looking at the four verbs.

To Know

From our previous studies, we determined that to "know" (*yada*) means we are "to know something in a completed sense; to know everything and to know fully; to learn to know. It means to know by intimate experience or expression; to choose, to approve, to love, to embrace, to desire, to place one's favor upon."[1] It's a deeply personal kind of knowledge forged by one's choice, affection, conviction and experience. Proverbs 1:2 says we are to "know" (*yada*) in an intimate, personal way, both "wisdom and instruction"— *wisdom* being more than the raw accumulation of facts. True wisdom refers to facts and convictions that have been reinforced by our choices and experiences. These facts, convictions, choices and experiences then determine what is a right and God-honoring course of action. *Instruction* is defined as "correction, discipline, and chastening, as a loving father disciplines his own son."[2]

God has provided for us, in His Son, both the wisdom of God (1 Cor. 1:30) and the steady hand of correction and discipline. He wants to make sure we know (*yada*) His Word and how to apply what we know (*yada*) in our everyday choices that will either bring Him glory or disrepute. Therefore, if you find yourself convicted and troubled by the words you read, rejoice! That's God's very intention. The Lord only chastises those He loves, as a father disciplines his own son.

> **Proverbs 3:11-12** - My son, do not despise the *chastening* of the LORD, nor detest His *correction*; (why) for whom the LORD loves He *corrects*, (to what extent) just as a father the son in whom he delights.

To Perceive

Next, we are to "*perceive* the words of understanding" (Prov. 1:2). To perceive (*biyn*) is "to discern, to observe, to have insight into, to consider diligently."[3] It involves more than mere head knowledge. To *perceive* is to have a truth suddenly become alive and real to us. It's as though our blinders are removed, or the fog clears, and we can see God's Word as never before.

We now see with 20/20 vision. The "words of understanding", or literally the "words of comprehension, discernment, righteous actions, with a strong moral and religious connotation", are in view. In other words, we now see clearly the holiness of God. We comprehend our sinfulness, God's perfection, and His wonderful gift of grace. By virtue of the indwelling of the Holy Spirit, we now have discernment to be able to choose what is true, noble, just, pure, lovely, of good report, virtuous, and praiseworthy (Phil. 4:8) and not follow our lusts or waste our lives living for the things that won't last. We can now clearly choose to "walk in the Spirit" and "not fulfill the lust of the flesh" (Gal. 5:16).

What a blessing it is to be able to *perceive* the things of God and then have the freedom and ability to choose to follow Him, no matter what.

To Receive

Knowing, even to the point of having an "a-ha" moment when you *perceive*, deep down, something overwhelming and potentially life-changing, is not enough. You have to then choose to *receive*, or "to take in, to lay hold of, to seize, to get or fetch, to acquire by any means possible"[4] what you now comprehend in a deeper fashion. You have to voluntarily choose to move from where you are to where the truth takes you. You have to open up yourself, make yourself vulnerable, humble yourself, and receive the "instruction (discipline, correction, chastening) of wisdom" (Prov. 1:3).

It's like salvation.

Just knowing facts about Jesus won't bring you into eternal fellowship with Him. You must *receive* Him into your life, on His terms, which are all or nothing. You must die. You must be crucified with Him, and He must live within you and through you (Gal. 2:20). You must follow His path (the narrow gate), and not the wide road of your own choosing (Matt. 7:13-14). He must be Lord, and not just your personal Savior whom you can call upon whenever you need Him to get you out of a jam (Rom. 10:9).

He's not your co-pilot. He's God Almighty, Creator of all, and Sovereign in all things.

If just *knowing* were enough, Satan would spend eternity in heaven. After all, he *knows* as fact what we believe by faith. He *knows* Jesus died and was raised from the dead. He was there, he saw, and the demons trembled (James 2:19). Yet Satan refuses to bow his knee in submission to Christ and declare Him as Lord (Phil. 2:9-11). This is the vital, all important part of receiving Jesus Christ on His terms.

What do we receive when we receive the "instruction of wisdom"? Solomon begins to expand our understanding of all that comes with God's wisdom by using the terms, "justice, judgment, and equity."

Justice is defined as "righteousness, or what is right, just or normal" with God. It means having a "right relation to an ethical or legal standard; to be right or straight."[5] In essence, it's understanding the commands and laws of God and then choosing to align our life, both internally and externally, to be in obedience to the Word of God. It's the desire and ability to now choose to serve Christ, rather than our flesh or the god of this fallen world. The ability to live according to our new nature, found in Christ, is just another gift given to us by the indwelling presence of the Holy Spirit (2 Cor. 5:17).

Remember the words of Jesus: "But why do you call Me 'Lord, Lord,' and not do the things which I say?" (Luke 6:46). All of creation must respond to this question because now, through the Holy Spirit, we have the ability, the freedom, and the power to choose to obey Christ. We can live, as promised in Proverbs, a life of *justice*, being in a "right relation" to the commands and person of Christ. All we have to do is choose the straight and narrow path (Matt. 7:13-14).

Is it hard? You bet. But the choice is simple.

Next, we choose to *receive* into our lives the instruction, correction and discipline of *judgment*. This word denotes the "act of deciding a legal case in a court or in litigation before judges." It deals with the "ability to make a correct *judgment* on human actions."[6]

Whoa. Hold on right there. One of the sincerely held convictions of our fallen, politically correct culture is not to judge. You don't judge me and I won't judge you. It's the old "don't ask, don't tell" mantra." In fact, these words of Jesus, taken totally out of context, are proclaimed as absolute truth by those who reject the rest of His words as truth: "Judge not, that you be not judged" (Matt. 7:1).

So how can a Christian receive the "instruction of judgment" and still find favor in the eyes of the world? You can't. You will have to resolve yourself to a life of turmoil, tribulation and persecution if you choose to live in the center of His will. Embrace the trials you'll face (James 1:2), because Jesus promised great blessings to those who suffer persecution for His name's sake. "Rejoice and be exceedingly glad, for great is your reward in heaven, for so they persecuted the prophets who were before you" (Matt. 5:12).

"All who desire to live godly in Christ Jesus will suffer persecution" (2 Tim. 3:12). There's no way around it. It's a given, a done deal. The only way to escape persecution is to *not* desire to live godly in Christ, which produces its own set of horrific consequences (Matt. 25:31-46). You don't want to go down that path.

With wisdom comes the ability to see what is right and wrong, good and evil, true and false. The "instruction of judgment" means being able to discern genuineness from hypocrisy, good fruit from bad fruit, and true prophets from false prophets— in others as well as within ourselves (Matt. 7:15-20). As you can imagine, this aspect of wisdom often brings the unintended consequences of being called judgmental, unloving, a hater, a bigot, narrow-minded, and much more. Hence, the warning from Jesus about suffering persecution for His name's sake.

Finally, in Christ we wisely receive the "instruction of equity." *Equity* is defined as "evenness, fairness, uprightness, straightness, smoothness"; it points to what is "just, correct, right and fair in speech or actions"[7] (Isa. 33:15). It's dealing with others as you would have them deal with you (Matt. 7:12). It's being fair, honest, noble and upright in everything. Equity is the overflow of a life found "in Christ."

To Give

The fourth verb points to a complex subject dealing with what we're to give and to whom. That's the topic we'll look at next time.

Getting Serious

1. Where are you in the process of obtaining wisdom?
2. Have you passed from simply knowing (*yada*) to now perceiving something deeper in the Word of God?
3. Has God begun to speak to you in a personal, profound way through His Word and the Holy Spirit? Have you ever had a *rhema* (a word from Him) meant only for you? If so, when was that, and what did He say?
4. Do you remember when you received Jesus as Lord? Can you describe what took place? What has your life with Him been like since that momentous day?
5. On a scale from 1 to 10, how would you rate God's wisdom in your life right now and in your decision making process? What was it yesterday? Are you growing in the wisdom of God? Is He more real to you today than in the past? If not, why not?

Next Step Challenge

Receiving the wisdom of God is tied to receiving Christ Jesus as Lord and the Holy Spirit coming as the guarantee of your future inheritance (Eph. 1:13-14). Write down your salvation experience. Include the time when you knew regeneration took place and your life became hidden with Christ in God (Col. 3:3). Also include your spiritual journey since salvation.

What have you learned about wisdom as you've walked with Christ? Have you personally experienced the process outlined in Proverbs 1:1-4 about *knowing*, *perceiving* and *receiving*? What was the actual context in which God revealed to you His wisdom? What was the outcome of that encounter?

If you haven't experienced any of this with the Lord, what do you think the explanation could be? Is He the problem? Does He show favoritism or partiality? Is He withholding something from you that He's freely giving to others?

Or could the problem be you? Is it possible that you have never experienced salvation and true saving faith?

Notes

1. Baker, W., & Carpenter, E. E. (2003). The complete word study dictionary: Old Testament (p. 420). Chattanooga, TN: AMG Publishers.
2. Ibid., 582.
3. Ibid., 129-130.
4. Ibid., 554-555.
5. Ibid., 938-939.
6. Ibid., 687-688.
7. Ibid., 605-606.

DAY EIGHT

Four Verbs— Part Two

To know wisdom and instruction,
to perceive the words of understanding,
to receive the instruction of wisdom, justice, judgment,
and equity; to give prudence to the simple,
to the young man knowledge and discretion.
Proverbs 1:2-4

IN THE PREVIOUS CHAPTER, we came across a few intriguing verbs: *know, perceive, receive* and *give* and also the nouns associated with those verbs: wisdom, instruction, understanding, justice, judgment, equity, knowledge and discretion.

Recall Proverbs 1:2-4:

To *know* wisdom and instruction,
To *perceive* the words of understanding,

To *receive* the instruction of wisdom, justice,
judgment and equity;
To *give* prudence to the simple (and to give) to the
young man knowledge and discretion.

Notice again the natural progression of action. First, to *know*.
Then to *perceive* something. After that to choose to personally
receive and embrace what we know and perceive. And finally, to
share or *give* to someone else what we have received.

We've already looked at the first three verbs. Now let's spend
some time trying to see and understand what the Lord expects us
to do with what we've received from Him, in Christ, by grace.

The answer to that question is found in one simple word: *give*.

What are we to *give* to others? And who are the *others* we are
to *give* something to?

To Give

Specifically, what are we to do with what we've received from
Him? We're to give it away. We're to give our lives to others.
This is the meaning of: "You shall love your neighbor as yourself"
(Matt. 22:39).

Question: What are we to actually give to others?
Answer: What we have received from Him: grace, love,
understanding, hope and wisdom.

Question: Who are we to share and give to?
Answer: Everyone. Especially the "simple" and the "young
man."

Look again at Proverbs 1:4: "To give prudence to (who) *the simple*, to the (who) *young man* knowledge and discretion." Four words stand out in this verse: prudence, simple, knowledge and discretion. We are to give *prudence*, meaning "shrewdness, cautiousness" to the simple. In fact, *prudence* can also be translated as "common sense, care, or good judgment."[1] The word *simple* means "naive, foolish, gullible, inexperienced or simpleminded"— pretty much the opposite of prudence.[2] It describes someone not firing on all cylinders, someone who doesn't have it all together, and someone lacking wisdom and common sense.

The book of Proverbs speaks much about the simpleminded person. For example:

> **Proverbs 1:22** - "How long, you *simple ones*, will you love *simplicity*? For scorners delight in their scorning, and fools hate knowledge."

> **Proverbs 7:7** - And (I) saw among the *simple*, I perceived among the youths, a young man devoid of understanding.

> **Proverbs 8:5** - "O you *simple ones*, understand prudence, and you fools, be of an understanding heart."

> **Proverbs 14:15** - The *simple* believes every word, but the prudent considers well his steps.

> **Proverbs 14:18** - The *simple* inherit folly, but the prudent are crowned with knowledge.

Proverbs 22:3 - A prudent man foresees evil and hides himself, but the *simple* pass on and are punished.

Therefore, we are to *give* (place before) the *simple* (the naive, the gullible, those lacking common sense, good judgment and discipline) *prudence*. We are to give to those lacking wisdom the same wisdom from God that we possess, in order to help them make good, God-honoring choices with their lives, so as to not be led astray into sin and its consequences. We can only do that by opening our mouth and speaking truth to those who might, or might not, appreciate what we're about to say. Their reaction does not really matter. All we should be concerned with is our obedience to *give* what we *know* and *perceive* and have *received*, by grace, from Him.

Again, note the progression. First, we *know* God's truth by experience and acceptance. Next, we *perceive* by our senses the impact of this profound truth concerning God's wisdom. Our eyes are now opened to the truth in a new and unmistakable way. Then, we must make it personal by choosing to *receive* what we now know and see into our lives. This demands obedience, which is an all or nothing commitment to what we know to be true. Finally, as Oswald Chambers said, we are to be willingly spent on others, "like broken bread and poured out wine." We are to *give* to others what we have received from Him by grace, especially to the most vulnerable of all people: the "simple" and the "young men."

The Young Men

Why did Solomon single out the "young men"? It's because they tend to be the most zealous, the strongest, the easiest to sway, and the people who need the most guidance. When we use the phrase, "he went off half-cocked" we are usually not referring to an older man, any woman, or a child. It's the young man, the punk, the headstrong, the "better get out of my way" man. It's "zeal without knowledge" on steroids. "Don't try to confuse me with the truth! I've already made up my mind."

> **Proverbs 19:2** - Also it is not good for a soul to be without *knowledge*, and he sins who hastens with his feet.

> **Romans 10:2-3** - For I bear them witness that they have a *zeal* for God, but not according to *knowledge*. For they being ignorant of God's righteousness, and seeking to establish their own righteousness, have not submitted to the righteousness of God.

What are we to give excited, passionate, yet sometimes misguided young men? Proverbs says we are to give them *knowledge* and *discretion* (understanding, insight, wisdom and a purposeful plan of application). It's the antidote for going off half-cocked, or saying, "I've just got to do something, even if it's wrong!" It's the opposite of calling your own shots or doing what seems best in your own eyes (Judges 21:25). Having "knowledge and discretion" is the ability to think clearly, without being overwhelmed by strong, confusing emotions. It means following the truth and the facts to a course of action that is true, noble, just, pure, lovely, of good report, virtuous and praiseworthy (Phil. 4:8). It's being "in Christ" and living in the wisdom of God.

Wisdom is the one thing that can save our younger generation today. Wisdom provides an understanding of life and the things of God; a *purpose* or plan in Him. God-ordained wisdom is what gives life meaning. Proverbs 7:7 says, "And (I) saw among the *simple*, I perceived among the youths, a *young man* devoid of (what) *understanding*." Yes, understanding. It's up to us to give to those He loves what we've already received in Him, by His grace.

The Four Verbs

Having wisdom, having the "mind of Christ" (1 Cor. 2:16), and having Christ Himself, who "became for us wisdom from God" (1 Cor. 1:30) involves responsibility. It's not something for us to miserly hoard or keep to ourselves. We're not independent contractors, free agents or lone wolves. Remember, we are the "light of the world" and "a city that is set on a hill." So "let your light so shine before men, that they may see your good works and glorify your Father in heaven" (Matt. 5:14-16). We are, like our Lord, to live for others and not ourselves.

Proverbs reveals to us the process of receiving the wisdom of God and shows us how to lovingly give it to others. We first *know*, next *perceive* inwardly, then choose to *receive* on His terms, and finally determine to *give*, no matter how uncomfortable that might make us feel. In doing so, we imitate the life of Christ to others (Eph. 5:1) and bring the Father glory.

Bringing God glory is what Jesus lived for. It should be our passion and the driving, pulsating purpose of our existence. Will you join me in this lifelong endeavor of receiving wisdom from God and then gladly, joyously giving it all away? Will you spend your life, like our Lord, serving others?

Getting Serious

1. How would you describe your ministry to others?
2. How would you describe your ministry to others who are not family members, friends, or members of your own church?
3. Is there a difference between your answer to Question 1 and Question 2? If so, why?
4. Do you believe the Lord has given you His wisdom? If so, how do you know? Did He bless you with His wisdom for you to be wise only to yourself or those you love? Or could there be something more He has in mind?
5. On a scale from 1 to 10, how would you rate God's wisdom in your life right now and in your decision making process? What was it yesterday? Are you growing in the wisdom of God? If not, why not?

Next Step Challenge

Use your Bible to look up the following verses. Read them in context and see what you can learn about your responsibilities to others as a Christian.

Mark 16:15 - And He said to them, "Go into all the world and preach the gospel to every creature."

Psalm 96:3 - "Declare His glory among the nations, His wonders among all peoples."

Revelation 14:6-8 - "Then I saw another angel flying in the midst of heaven, having the everlasting gospel to preach to those who dwell on the earth— to every nation, tribe, tongue, and people— saying with a loud voice, 'Fear God and give glory to Him, for the hour of His judgment has come; and worship Him who made heaven and earth, the sea and springs of water.'"

How do these verses apply to you? Are you to declare His glory and wonders among the people?

If God proclaims His Word by angels in the future, how will He use you today to do the same?

What are you prepared to do about it?

Notes

1. Baker, W., & Carpenter, E. E. (2003). The complete word study dictionary: Old Testament (p. 874). Chattanooga, TN: AMG Publishers.

2. Ibid., 930.

DAY NINE

Are You a Wise Guy?

A wise man will hear and increase learning,
and a man of understanding will attain wise counsel,
to understand a proverb and an enigma,
the words of the wise and their riddles.
Proverbs 1:5-6

A S WE LEARNED FROM OUR LAST study together, Solomon has some pointed words to say to simple and impetuous young men.

> **Proverbs 1:4** - To give prudence to the *simple* (and to give) to the *young man* knowledge and discretion.

Solomon also has much to say to the wise and learned men of understanding who seek godly counsel. Proverbs is a book given to us through the inspiration of the Holy Spirit (2 Tim. 3:16). It's for all of us: the young, the old, the dedicated as well as the apathetic, the hot, the cold and the lukewarm (Rev. 3:15-17). It's for the theologically trained as well as the ones who only know one thing: "Though I was blind, now I see." (John 9:25). It's for everyone. Regardless of our sinful, broken past or our life of privilege and opulence, the wisdom of God— revealed in Proverbs— calls each of us, no matter who we are, into a deeper relationship with Him.

In the closing two verses of the preamble to this grand gift to us, Solomon lets the pendulum swing hard to the other side and turns his attention to the opposite of the simple and naive. He now addresses the wise and astute (the ones who *should* know better; who *do* know better) and shows us how to understand the book of Proverbs.

Let's take a look at what Solomon has to say to those who live on the other end of the continuum.

The Wisdom of the Wise

In Proverbs 1:5-6 we read:

> A wise man will hear and increase learning, and a
> man of understanding will attain wise counsel, to
> understand a proverb and an enigma, the words of
> the wise and their riddles.

In this passage, Solomon is addressing two categories of people: a *wise man* and a *man of understanding.* Who are these people and what about their character draws us to them?

The Wise Man

The term *wise man* is used to describe "one who is skilled or experienced."[1] Proverbs expands this definition by showing a *wise man* to be one who continues to learn and is teachable (Prov. 9:9, 13:1), one who heeds and accepts a rebuke (Prov. 9:8, 15:31), and one who speaks properly (Prov. 14:3, 15:2, 16:23). Solomon continually contrasts the life of the wise man with the foolish man in an effort to show us the inevitable results of the choices we make. For example:

> **Proverbs 3:35** - The *wise* shall inherit glory, *but* shame shall be the legacy of fools.

> **Proverbs 10:8** - The *wise* in heart will receive commands, *but* a prating fool will fall.

> **Proverbs 10:14** - *Wise* people store up knowledge, *but* the mouth of the foolish is near destruction.

A *wise man* is only wise because he has received the wisdom from God that makes him wise. His wisdom does not come from within himself, a university degree, or his apparent success in this world. Scripture tells us that all the wisdom this world can offer is "foolishness (moronic, folly, absurdity)[2] in God's sight" (1 Cor. 3:19 NIV) and will soon fade away. It means nothing. Zilch.

Proverbs 1:5 begins by telling us the "wise man will *hear* (listen, be attentive, understand, obey)[3] and, as a result of hearing, *increase* (do again, add, continue)[4] *learning* (receive teaching, insight, instruction)."⁵ The wise man thirsts for more, wants more, and craves more. He will not be satisfied with trifle tidbits of information designed to placate his curiosity. He's inquisitive, with an insatiable appetite for more than what he's already received. "If there's more to Christ than what I know right now, I want it! And I won't be satisfied with anything less."

The wise man— the one filled with the wisdom of God, with Christ Himself (1 Cor. 1:30), will *hear*, listen, understand, and then obey what he receives from the Lord. He will be loyal and trustworthy. He will be faithful with the little he has, knowing Christ will soon reward him with greater truths (Luke 16:10). The more he *sees* of Jesus, the more he *understands* about Jesus. The more he *lives* in the unbroken presence of Jesus, the more he *wants* Jesus. Nothing else matters. Nothing else can satisfy.

A wise man will *hear* from the Lord and then *increase* or continue in what he has *learned*. He wants to know more, experience more and understand more. He will study the Scriptures to present himself "approved to God, a worker who does not need to be ashamed, rightly dividing the word of truth" (2 Tim. 2:15). He will diligently memorize Scripture in order to hide God's word in his heart, that he might not sin against God (Psalm 119:11), and he will work hard to grow in the wisdom God has provided him (Prov. 9:9).

A Man of Understanding

On the other hand, a "man of understanding" (*biyn*) is a man of "comprehension and discernment; one who exhibits righteous actions with a strong moral and religious connotation."⁶ He's a man who strives after the things of God and who can discern the difference between, not only the "good" and the "bad", but also the "good" and the "best."

Proverbs says "a man of understanding will *attain* wise counsel" (Prov. 1:5). The word *attain* means to "get, buy, possess"[7] at all cost and is reminiscent of the kingdom parables spoken by our Lord. A man finds a treasure hidden in a field and joyfully goes and sells all he has to purchase the field (Matt. 13:44). Why? To *attain* the treasure, no matter the cost. A merchant seeking beautiful pearls finds what he's looking for and sells all he has to buy the pearl— the object of his search and obviously the passion of his life (Matt. 13:45-46). He will not let anything keep him from attaining the pearl, even if it costs him all he has. So it is with the "man of understanding" when it comes to getting *wise counsel*.

The phrase *wise counsel* means wise "guidance, direction, or good advice."[8] The importance of this virtue is taught in many places throughout the book of Proverbs. For example:

> **Proverbs 11:14** - Where there is no *counsel*, the people fall; but in the multitude of *counselors* there is safety.

> **Proverbs 12:15** - The way of a fool is right in his own eyes, but he who heeds *counsel* is wise.

> **Proverbs 13:10** - By pride comes nothing but strife, but with the *well-advised* is wisdom.

> **Proverbs 20:18** - Plans are established by *counsel*; by *wise counsel* wage war.

Proverbs 24:6 - For by *wise counsel* you will wage your own war, and in a multitude of *counselors* there is safety.

A "man of understanding" seeks *wise counsel* in order to learn from others who have also received the wisdom of God. Wise counsel leads to collective wisdom. No one man can know everything there is to know about all things. After all, "he who walks with wise men will be wise" (Prov. 13:20). A "wise man is strong, yes, a man of knowledge increases strength" (Prov. 24:5).

Riddles and Dark Sayings

Let's look again at the last part of Proverbs 1:6. What about the "riddles and dark sayings"?[9] It seems the "wise man" and the "man of understanding" will "hear and increase learning" and "attain wise counsel" for only one reason: "to understand a proverb and an enigma, the words of the wise and their riddles."

What is an enigma and the words of the wise and their riddles? Hold on, because we will look into that next time.

Until then, enjoy some wise sayings from our own culture:

"Two minds are better than one."

"Many hands make light work."

"When spider webs unite, they can tie up a lion."

Getting Serious

1. How would you describe your quiet time with the Lord?
2. Do you have a special place where you meet daily with the Lord? Does He meet you there? If so, what is your time with Him like?
3. Do you have a group of fellow believers who speak wisdom into your life? If so, how did you meet them? How has your intimacy and trust with them grown over time?
4. If you don't have other believers in your life who can offer you wise counsel, why is that? Are you a person who is in a position to offer wise counsel to others? If so, how did these relationships come about? If not, why not?
5. On a scale from 1 to 10, how would you rate God's wisdom in your life right now and in your decision making process? What was it yesterday? Are you growing in the wisdom of God? If not, why not?

Next Step Challenge

Get a sheet of paper and write down five people you know to be wise and ones from whom you would trust to receive counsel. What is it about their lives that leads you to trust them? What character traits do they possess that you admire the most? What single thing in their life speaks loudest about their relationship with Christ?

Do you have the same character traits in your life that you admire in theirs? If not, what are you prepared to do about it? Are you willing to humble yourself before the Lord and ask Him to change you into the person He wants you to be, no matter the cost? Have you asked God for His wisdom, found in His Son? Have you received Jesus on His terms?

Finally, make a list of five people you would never go to for wise advice. List the reasons why. Then compare the two lists and see which one most describes your own character traits.

Is the news good or bad? What are you prepared to do about it?

Notes

1. Baker, W., & Carpenter, E. E. (2003). The complete word study dictionary: Old Testament (pp. 336–337). Chattanooga, TN: AMG Publishers.
2. Zodhiates, S. (2000). The complete word study dictionary: New Testament (p. 1001). Chattanooga, TN: AMG Publishers.
3. Baker, 1166-1167.
4. Ibid., 453-454.
5. Ibid., 555.
6. Ibid., 129-130.
7. Ibid., 1001.
8. Ibid., 1221-1222.
9. The phrase, "riddles and dark sayings" is another translation of the Hebrew word *enigma* (*mĕlîytsah*). We will look more deeply at *enigma* in the next chapter.

DAY TEN

Riddles and Dark Sayings

A wise man will hear and increase learning,
and a man of understanding will attain wise counsel,
to understand a proverb and an enigma,
the words of the wise and their riddles.
Proverbs 1:5-6

SOLOMON IS READY TO CLOSE OUT the preamble to the book of Proverbs in a surprising way. Proverbs 1:5 tells us that one of the primary purposes of this book, and of wisdom itself, is to allow us to "hear and increase learning (to receive teaching, insight, instruction)"[1] and to "attain (get, buy, possess, no matter the costs)[2] wise counsel (wise guidance, direction, or good advice)."[3]

We already know that we need wise counsel. But we have not discussed the actual reason for it.

Why do we need wise counsel? What's the purpose or the pay-off for us in real time? What's out there that's so important to learn, to understand, and to have insight into? What about the last part of this passage— the "riddles and dark sayings"? It seems that the "wise man" and the "man of understanding" will "hear and increase learning" and "attain wise counsel" for only one reason: "to understand a proverb and an enigma, the words of the wise and their riddles" (Prov. 1:6).

The Climax of the Definition of Wisdom

A truly wise man is not one who has already attained wisdom, but one who's keenly aware that he hasn't attained it yet. He is desperately striving to be more like Christ, or to "press on, that I may lay hold of that for which Christ Jesus has also laid hold of me" (Phil. 3:12). He's one who's not satisfied with the spiritual status quo and is not content with his Bible College diploma, signifying he has learned all there is to know about Christ and His Word. The wise man longs to dig deeper, to pray harder, to speak louder, to shine brighter, and to love more intensely than he thought humanly possible.

To this *wise man*, to the *man of understanding* comes one of the greatest blessings of all. He, by virtue of the wisdom given him by the indwelling presence of the Holy Spirit, will learn to "understand a proverb and an enigma, the words of the wise and their riddles" (Prov. 1:6). To him, the doors of the deeper truths of the things of God are opened and he is graciously invited to come and dine.

We know the meaning of *proverb*, but what's an "enigma"? And what's all this about the "words of the wise and their riddles"?

An enigma (*měliytsah*) is translated as "a person or thing that is mysterious, puzzling, or difficult to understand." Admittedly, it's a difficult word to translate in this proverb. It can also mean a "riddle", a "symbol or parable", a "discourse requiring an interpretation", or simply "a figurative and involved discourse" that is closely related to the phrase "riddles and dark sayings."[4] When rendered together, these words point to something obscure in meaning, or to some truth that is difficult to uncover and understand.

How do we know this? By looking at the meaning of "riddles" or "dark sayings." The word translated here is *hiydah* and means "difficult questions, perplexing sayings, a statement with a double meaning, or dark and obscure utterances."[5] It seems to be speaking about truths that are not on the surface for everyone to see. The truths are more hidden, like buried treasure. Only a diligent, wise person will know to dig for them, and then value them when found.

According to Proverbs, this is the climax, the zenith and the pinnacle of wisdom. It doesn't get any better than being able to understand the mysterious, puzzling, profoundly deep things of God that change us forever. "As the heavens are higher than the earth, so are My ways higher than your ways, and My thoughts than your thoughts" says the Lord (Isa. 55:9). Maybe, just maybe, we can catch a fleeting glimpse of how high His thoughts actually are. What an incredible blessing! Tell me what compares to having the "mind of Christ" (1 Cor. 2:16)?

Ears to Hear

Jesus hinted of this when He used the cryptic phrase, "He who has ears to hear, let him hear" before speaking profound truth to only those who were able to receive it. These words were not FPC (For Public Consumption). They were only for those who understood the implications of what the Lord was saying. Only the wise could understand Jesus' parables, His stories with their hidden meaning, and the mysterious, deep, dark sayings of the Lord.

Let's look at a few of these.

When talking about John the Baptist, Jesus said he was the greatest man who ever lived and the last of the Old Testament prophets (Matt. 11:11-13). Then He threw the crowd a curve. He said, "And if you are willing to receive it, he is Elijah who is to come" (Matt. 11:14). Note the *if* in His statement. Not everyone was willing to receive John as coming in the spirit of Elijah. According to Malachi in the last two verses of the Old Testament, Elijah was to come as the forerunner of the Christ, the Messiah (Mal. 4:5-6). John was the forerunner of Jesus. So if they received what Jesus said about John, they would have to conclude that Jesus was the Messiah, the Son of God, and the Holy One of Israel.

But not everyone was willing to do that. Therefore, the truth He uttered was not for everyone, but only for a few. It was for the chosen, the elect, and the ones with believing hearts. Hence, Jesus said, "He who has ears to hear, let him (not everyone else) hear" (Matt. 11:15).

When Jesus preached His powerful and far reaching parable about the sower and the seeds, He ended it by saying, "He who has ears to hear, let him (not everyone) hear" (Mark 4:9). Why? Because this parable deals with true salvation and the deception of non-saving faith. It paints a vivid picture of those who are holding on to traditions, or the teachings of men. They are enamored with Christ for a short while, compared to what true salvation looks like. True salvation always involves fruit, and not mere profession (Matt. 7:15-20). It's an utterly profound teaching that not everyone receives or understands. It's for the few, the chosen, the elect, and the ones "who have ears to hear."

We see these cryptic, mysterious, dark sayings of Jesus when He spoke about life in the kingdom (Matt. 13:9). He also used these words after confronting the Pharisees about their religious and spiritual hypocrisy (Mark 7:16). When He told His disciples the true cost of discipleship: "So, likewise, whoever of you does not forsake all that he has cannot be My disciple" (Luke 14:33), He ended that teaching with the same puzzling words: "He who has ears to hear, let him hear!" (Luke 14:35). Those with "ears to hear" were not puzzled by what Jesus said. It was the others, the masses, the everyone else who were totally confused.

Jesus ends each of His seven letters to the seven churches (Revelation 2 and 3) the same way: "He who has an ear, let him hear what the Spirit says to the churches" (Rev. 2:7, 11, 17, 29; 3:6, 13, 22). If there was ever a book of the Bible full of enigmas, riddles and dark sayings, it is the book of Revelation.

Back to the Dark Sayings

We have been given, as a great and precious gift, the privilege of being able to understand and comprehend the deeper things of God (the sometimes confusing, puzzling and mysterious aspects of His being). He has granted us, as mere mortals, insights into the eternal. These great insights are the things that "many prophets and righteous men desired to see, and did not see" (Matt. 13:17). They have been given to each of us by the indwelling presence of the Holy Spirit, who is the Sovereign One Himself.

With the wisdom of God we can "understand a proverb and an enigma, the words of the wise and their riddles" (Prov. 1:6).

All we have to do is *use* what is now *ours*. Einstein once said, "It's not that I'm so smart, it's just that I stay with the problems longer." In other words, I do the work. I put in the time. I stay focused and committed until I find the answer. The same can be said regarding wisdom and the child of God, just as long as we *use* what is now *ours* to use.

Do Not Forsake Your Inheritance

One of the most tragic stories in all of Scripture is the account of Esau trading his blessed inheritance for a bowl of stew— for one meager can of Dinty Moore stew (Gen. 25:33-34). How could he do such a thing? The same way we do. How could he have been so short-sighted, foolish and just plain stupid? The same way we are. We do it all the time.

Solomon has revealed to us one of the blessings of wisdom— of knowing the Lord in an intimate, personal way. By virtue of God's wisdom imparted to us, we become wise. One of the blessings of being a wise man is the ability to understand and discern the wondrous and mysterious things in the Word of God that reveal God Himself to us. Our inheritance is to have the indescribable privilege of calling Him "Abba, Father" and of Him seeing us as His children, His sons, and as members of His family (Rom. 8:15). Furthermore, our blessed inheritance means we are also "heirs of God and joint heirs with Christ" (Rom. 8:17).

Is there anything you would trade for your inheritance?

If you say " absolutely nothing", then great! But our lives and our affections often tell a different story. We do what we want to do and serve who we want to serve. Jesus put it this way, "For where your treasure is, there your heart will be also" (Matt. 6:21). If we treasure our life in the here and now and what this fallen world thinks of us or promises to give us, our hearts have drifted far from the inheritance that's ours and the kingdom which is our home. Wisdom is no longer our desire. The "dark sayings" of the Lord remain dark, hidden and concealed by a veil of our own apathy. How sad.

We have a promise and an inheritance. Beware, lest you fall into the same trap as Esau and forfeit everything for eternity because you want something that tastes good right now.

The spiritual life with Christ is a marathon. It isn't a sprint. Be committed for the long haul and strive, with all you are, to be a wise man that understands what others call "riddles, an enigma, and dark sayings."

Be this kind of man or woman, even if you stand alone.

Final Question

The promise sounds wonderfully appealing. But where do we begin? What's the first step? It's one thing to talk about the blessings of wisdom and then dangle them out in front of us, like a carrot before a horse. It's quite another to provide us with a roadmap, a guide book of some sort, or maybe an instruction manual to point us in the right direction. Otherwise, Solomon would leave us frustrated about seeing the goal and having no clue how to get there.

Fortunately, there's good news: "The fear of the Lord is the beginning of knowledge, but fools despise wisdom and instruction" (Prov. 1:7). What a contrast! We just need to figure out exactly what the "fear of the Lord" means and we should be on our way.

As Julie Andrews sang in the Sound of Music, "Let's start at the very beginning, a very good place to start."

For us, that beginning is the "fear of the Lord."

Getting Serious

1. When was the last time God spoke to you and revealed something He had previously kept hidden from you?
2. Do you know why He kept that part of Himself from you? Was it Him? Or was the reason something in you?
3. Do you believe it's actually possible to have the kind of relationship with the Father that He would be pleased to share His heart with you? Does your faith stretch that far? Or do you think this is just an unobtainable goal?
4. If you answered, *yes* to the last question, are you willing to put in the time and effort to have this kind of relationship with the Lord? Do you know how to begin? Do you know a person who God currently shares His heart with?
5. On a scale from 1 to 10, how would you rate God's wisdom in your life right now and in your decision making process? What was it yesterday? Are you growing in the wisdom of God? If not, why not?

Next Step Challenge

Using your Bible, look up every time the Lord spoke the words, "He who has ears to hear, let him hear" and write them down. Then spend some time reading them in context. What was the Lord trying to say when He spoke these words?

Do you understand His message and the implications of what He is teaching? Do His words have any impact on your life right now? Is there something He is trying to say to you when you read His words?

Do you have ears to hear? If so, do you hear what He is saying to you right now?

Notes

1. Baker, W., & Carpenter, E. E. (2003). The complete word study dictionary: Old Testament (p. 555). Chattanooga, TN: AMG Publishers.
2. Ibid., 1001.
3. Ibid., 1221-1222.
4. Ibid., 617.
5. Ibid., 332.

PART TWO

Teach me Your way, O LORD; I will walk in Your truth;
unite my heart to fear Your name.

Psalm 86:11

"And do not fear those who kill the body but cannot kill the soul.
But rather fear Him who is able to destroy both
soul and body in hell."

Matthew 10:28

DAY ELEVEN

The Beginning of the Beginning

The fear of the LORD is the beginning of knowledge,
but fools despise wisdom and instruction.
Proverbs 1:7

EVERYTHING HAS A BEGINNING, a first start, or a genesis. Everything begins somewhere. According to Proverbs, there's a beginning to knowledge, wisdom and instruction. That glorious beginning is called "the fear of the Lord" (Prov. 1:7).

What does it mean to "fear the Lord"? If "God is love" as the Scriptures say (1 John 4:8), how are we to fear His love, His mercy, His grace, or any other aspect of His character? How can the fear of the Lord be the beginning of anything but a dysfunctional relationship? Are we to be so frightened that we cower in His presence? Fear is not a pleasant emotion that draws us closer to the one we fear. So why would the Lord tell us the fear of Him, rather than the love of Him, is the starting point of knowledge and wisdom?

What Does Fear Really Mean?

Our English definition of *fear* reads like this: "an unpleasant emotion caused by the belief that someone or something is dangerous, likely to cause pain, or is a threat." Fear is also described as the "anticipation of the possibility that something unpleasant will occur."[1] You know: the *fear* of financial ruin, the *fear* of heights, the *fear* for one's safety, or the *fear* of speaking in public. There are countless ways to describe fear as an unpleasant emotion, caused by the possibility of something bad happening to us.

In the Scriptures, *fear* has an added connotation. In addition to the idea of God Himself being "an awesome, terrifying, and fearful thing", to "fear the Lord" means to "honor, respect, and be in awe" of Him.[2] In other words, the "fear of the Lord" means to show profound respect, while recognizing that the object of our fear is "awesome and terrifying". He can bless or crush us at any time, for any reason, at His own whim, without recourse. He is the Creator, the Highest Authority, and the Sovereign One. And we are mere mortals— just dust and ashes.

Having a healthy "fear of the Lord" should motivate us to please Him in all that we do. We will someday have to give an account to Him for what we've done, whether good or bad or indifferent, while living our lives on this earth (2 Cor. 5:10). He will be our Judge and the final Arbiter of our fate. He will judge us according to His infallible standard of righteousness and holiness, and not by our lukewarm platitudes, designed to excuse our apathy.

The First Door Opened

The final promise made to us in the preamble to the Proverbs reads:

> **Proverbs 1:5-6** - A wise man will hear and increase learning, and a man of understanding will attain wise counsel, (why) to understand a proverb and an enigma, the words of the wise and their riddles (dark, hidden sayings).

What's the first enigma (the first strange, dark saying) we are to understand? What door has the promise of wisdom opened to us first?

It's the importance of the "fear of the Lord"— or more literally, "the fear of Jehovah" (Prov. 1:7). This "fear of the Lord" is the foundation upon which our future relationship with God is formed.

The word *fear* is like a two-edged sword. On one side of the blade is engraved the words "Respect, Honor, Awe and Reverence", while the other side reads "Fright, Terror, Dread and Great Fear." They're both part of the same sword. They're both key attributes of the character of God. They're not contradictory in nature, nor mutually exclusive. God is both merciful and just. He is ever forgiving, but ultimately holds us accountable for our sins. He is loving, gracious and good, yet incredibly fearful and terrifying at the same time.

The first enigma we're to understand is a seemingly illogical one. It states that the *fear* (dually defined as profound reverence and terrifying dread) *of the Lord is the beginning*, the inception, or the starting place *of knowledge*, discernment and insight into the things of God.

That's a good thing.

You see, we have this nagging tendency to view the God revealed in the Old Testament and Jesus as two totally different beings. The Old Testament God seems fearful, terrifying, capricious and often unapproachable. He came with fire, thunder and lightning on Mt. Sinai, causing the Jews to quake in fear, like the cowardly lion did when meeting the Wizard of Oz. The Old Testament God is seen as the God of curses, judgment, plagues and wrath while the New Testament God (Jesus) is viewed as loving, patient and forgiving, full of mercy and grace. Jesus understands us. He's like us in many ways, or so we'd like to think. He's approachable and not judgmental, like a close friend or best buddy. We can do anything we want and He will just smile, wink, and turn a blind eye because He loves us and only wants to make us happy.

The Old Testament God? Not so much.

See One, See All

The Father, God and Jesus, the Son are actually one and the same. Jesus said, "He who has seen Me has seen the Father" (John 14:9). He also said, "I and My Father are one" (John 10:30). To view Jesus as a cosmic sidekick or good buddy and ignore the fact that He is God, Sovereign over all, the Creator (John 1:3), and the Sustainer (Heb. 1:3) of everything, opens a door that leads us away from wisdom and into the murky waters of self-deception. We tend to love the Jesus we've created in our own image and fear the God of the Old Testament who we don't fully understand, nor really want to. Why? Because we don't like fear. Not one bit.

Fear causes us to have to watch what we say, to guard our hearts, and to constantly be aware of the sin in our lives. Fear makes us feel uncomfortable and troubled, because of the *object* of our fear. We fear the Law Enforcement Officer when we see his blue lights in our rear view mirror because of the hardship a speeding ticket causes. We fear our boss when we stand outside his office door, nervously knocking, knowing he wants to see us immediately and we haven't a clue as to why. We fear the IRS when their letter questions some fuzzy deduction on our tax return that we didn't feel so good about when we filed it last April. These *objects* of our fear have an element of power and control over our lives that can bring us some pain. There's not much we can do about it but complain.

We fear what the officer, or our boss, or the IRS can do to us for our non-compliance to what is required, so we give them great respect, and we honor their authority. Why? Because we don't want to make things worse for ourselves by making them mad. We fear their authority and the power they have over our lives. That's why we put on our Sunday smile and treat them as nice as we possibly can. We are careful to never defend ourselves or demean them for doing their job.

"Oh, excuse me officer. I'm so sorry I was speeding. Thank you for the ticket. Have a great day."

"Sir, is there something you wanted to see me about? Is there something I can do to help you?"

We answer all their questions and suffer through all their demands with a polite, "Sir" and "Yes, Sir" regardless of how we feel. They have the power, for that moment at least, to cause us happiness or pain, and to make us rejoice or suffer. It's their power, by virtue of their position and authority that we respect and fear, even if we don't respect the individual person holding that position.

If it is true of a highway cop and a $360 speeding ticket, how much more should it be true if the *object* of our fear is the Lord Himself?

Fear is the Beginning

There's no "Jesus we like, because He cuts us slack for our sin" and "God we don't like, because He's such a stickler for right and wrong." Or, "Jesus we love, because He loves us. But we don't like to hang around God that much, because He's always reminding us of how poorly we're doing in this life of holiness."

But there's not a choice. You can't be on one team and not on the other.

Jesus and the Father, the God of the Old Testament and the God of the New Testament, are one and the same. They are identical and of the same essence. We're to love the Father as much as the Son. We're to fear both the Father and the Son. It's a two way street. Love and fear flow both ways.

Jesus is not only forgiving, but also commands us unquestionably, just like the Father. His words to the woman caught in the act of adultery were first forgiving: "Woman, where are those accusers of yours? Has no one condemned you?" She said, "No one, Lord." And Jesus said to her, "Neither do I condemn you." Then He commanded: "Go and sin no more" (John 8:10-11).

Again, love and fear flow both ways.

For those who still see Jesus as always loving and God as always judgmental, consider the following passage of Scripture:

Revelation 6:15-17 - And the kings of the earth, the great men, the rich men, the commanders, the mighty men, every slave and every free man, hid themselves in the caves and in the rocks of the mountains, and said to the mountains and rocks, "Fall on us and hide us from the face of Him who sits on the throne and from the wrath of the Lamb! For the great day of His wrath has come, and who is able to stand?"

They were begging the rocks and mountains to fall on them in a vain attempt to hide from the "wrath of the Lamb" (Rev. 6:17). The Lamb is Jesus, and His wrath is coming.

Fear Only One

The book of Revelation is directly related to the book of Proverbs in that the *fear of the Lord*, and not of anything else, *is the beginning*, the source, and the starting place *of* all *knowledge*, wisdom, insight and discernment. It's our profound respect and honor, based on Who He is as our Sovereign Creator and Lord, that opens the door of deeper understanding to the things of God. It's our fear and terrifying dread of His authority and judgment that prompt us to live a life worthy of being called His children, as well as joint heirs with His Son (Rom. 8:16-17).

Fear is a healthy emotion to have towards the Lord. Look how Jesus addressed the subject.

Luke 12:4-5 - "And I say to you, My friends, do not be afraid of those who kill the body, and after that have no more that they can do. But I will

show you whom you should fear: Fear Him who,
after He has killed, has power to cast into hell; yes,
I say to you, fear Him!"

Who do you think Jesus was talking about? Who has the
power to cast one into hell? Satan? No. It's only God Himself.
It's a fear of Him alone that opens the door to the deeper truths
of the things of God.

"The fear of the Lord is the beginning of knowledge"
(Proverbs 1:7).

Getting Serious

1. Have you ever thought of Jesus as Someone you could trust, and Someone you wanted near you, but not God the Father?
2. When you pray to God, do you pray to the Father or to the Son? Do you pray to the Holy Spirit? Or do you simply use the generic phrase, Lord? Why do you think you choose to pray to the One that you do?
3. Does the thought of having fear for the Lord make you feel uncomfortable? Does it seem unnatural and maybe out of character? If so, why do you think you feel this way?
4. When you read the statement, "the fear of the Lord", is your first thought of profound respect and honor or do you think more of dread and terror? Does the phrase "fear of the Lord" have a positive meaning to you or a negative one? What about your perception of God leads you to either a positive or negative conclusion?
5. On a scale from 1 to 10, how would you rate God's wisdom in your life right now and in your decision making process? What was it yesterday? Are you growing in the wisdom of God? If not, why not?

Next Step Challenge

Using your Bible, do a search of the book of Proverbs and pick out all the times the phrase "fear of the Lord" is used. Write down the references. What is the Lord trying to say to you in these passages? What definition of *fear* is being used? Is it "terror and dread", or "profound respect and honor", or is it both? Now that you understand the meaning of *fear*, has your perception of God changed?

Look at the following passages and try to determine, in context, the definition of fear. How does the definition change, if at all, the meaning of what is being said?

> **1 Samuel 11:7** - So he took a yoke of oxen and cut them in pieces, and sent them throughout all the territory of Israel by the hands of messengers, saying, "Whoever does not go out with Saul and Samuel to battle, so it shall be done to his oxen." And *the fear of the LORD* fell on the people, and they came out with one consent.

> **2 Chronicles 17:10** - And the *fear of the LORD* fell on all the kingdoms of the lands that were around Judah, so that they did not make war against Jehoshaphat.

> **2 Chronicles 19:9** - And he commanded them, saying, "Thus you shall act in *the fear of the LORD*, faithfully and with a loyal heart."

> **Isaiah 33:6** - Wisdom and knowledge will be the stability of your times, and the strength of salvation; *the fear of the LORD* is His treasure.

> **Acts 9:31** - Then the churches throughout all Judea, Galilee, and Samaria had peace and were edified. And walking in *the fear of the Lord* and in

the comfort of the Holy Spirit, they were multiplied.

Do you have the fear of the Lord? If so, what is it like? How has it changed your life and your understanding and love of the Lord? If you don't have the fear of the Lord, why do you think that is? Does not having the fear of the Lord bring you fear?

It should, you know. It really should.

Notes

1. Fear. (1989) In Oxford English Dictionary online (2nd ed.), Retrieved from http://dictionary.com.
2. Baker, W., & Carpenter, E. E. (2003). The complete word study dictionary: Old Testament (p. 471). Chattanooga, TN: AMG Publishers.

DAY TWELVE

The Life of a Fool

The fear of the LORD is the beginning of knowledge,
but fools despise wisdom and instruction.
Proverbs 1:7

I N PROVERBS, WE ARE PRESENTED with the contrast
between two types of individuals: the wise man and the fool.
We've already seen how the "wise man will hear and increase
learning" and how a "man of understanding will attain wise
counsel" (Prov. 1:5). Now we're introduced to the man who lives
at the other end of the spectrum, on the other side of the tracks—
the fool.

What is a fool?

How does one become a fool?

And what is it about a fool that compels him to "despise
wisdom and instruction"? (Prov. 1:7).

The Fool Defined

When we use the term *fool* today, we think of someone who acts unwisely or imprudently, such as a silly person who tries to dupe, trick or prank us. We often equate the term with being stupid, simple or naive. The word *fool*, as used in Proverbs, has a much more sinister meaning.

In Proverbs 1:7, the Hebrew word for *fool* is *eviyl.* It means "foolish in the sense of one who hates wisdom and walks in folly by despising wisdom and morality." It describes one who "mocks when found guilty, one who is continually quarrelsome, and one who is licentious in his behavior."[1]

Proverbs declares that "fools hate knowledge" (Prov. 1:22) and "fools die for lack of wisdom" (Prov. 10:21). The heart of a fool, the very center of their being, "proclaims foolishness" (Prov. 12:23). "It is an abomination to fools (against their nature) to depart from evil" and do what is right (Prov. 13:19). Fools "mock at sin" (Prov. 14:9). Their mouth not only "feeds on foolishness" but "pours forth foolishness" (Prov. 15:14, 2) like a flood.

Therefore, one who lives and thinks this way naturally despises any "wisdom and instruction" that points out errors in their actions or lifestyle. "The foolishness of a man twists (perverts) his way, and his heart frets (is enraged) against the Lord" (Prov. 19:3). Consequently, the "way of a fool is right in his own eyes" (Prov. 12:15). You can "grind a fool in a mortar with a pestle along with crushed grain, yet his foolishness will not depart from him" (Prov. 27:22). His foolishness is embedded in his nature. It's part of his DNA. It's in the marrow of his bones.

Even so, there's more to being a *fool* than just a rejection of the truth found in Scripture. The verse also states that fools "despise" both the "wisdom and instruction" of God. Despise is a strong word. It means to "hold in contempt, to deem insignificant, and to show scorn or disrespect for someone or something."[2]

Putting this all together, Proverbs 1:7 reads:

> **Proverbs 1:7** - The *fear* (awe, profound reverence, terror and dread) of the LORD is the *beginning* (starting point, inception, genesis) of *knowledge* (discernment and insight into the things of God), *but* (the contrast) *fools* (those who mock when they are found guilty in their sin; those who are licentious, promiscuous and unprincipled in sexual matters and who live immoral lives) *despise* (scorn, disrespect, ridicule and view as insignificant and worthless) *wisdom* (the ability to discern and judge what is right, true, and lasting) and *instruction* (discipline, chastening, and correction, with the imagery of a father disciplining his son that he loves).

This truth is so important that Proverbs 23:9 restates it as such: "Do not speak in the hearing of a fool, (why) for he will *despise the wisdom of your words.*"

The Fool More Clearly Defined

The Scriptures, especially in Proverbs, have much more to say about the *fool*. In fact, the Lord gives us almost an entire chapter to show, in graphic detail, the life and future of a fool. Look what He says in Proverbs 26:1-12 and note the contrast between the wise and the fool:

As snow in summer and rain in harvest, so honor is not fitting for a *fool*.

Like a flitting sparrow, like a flying swallow, so a curse without cause shall not alight.

A whip for the horse, a bridle for the donkey, and a rod for the *fool's* back.

Do not answer a *fool* according to his *folly*, (why) lest you also be like him.

Answer a *fool* according to his *folly*, lest he be wise in his own eyes.

He who sends a message by the hand of a *fool* cuts off his own feet and drinks violence.

Like the legs of the lame that hang limp is a proverb in the mouth of *fools*.

Like one who binds a stone in a sling is he who gives honor to a *fool*.

Like a thorn that goes into the hand of a drunkard is a proverb in the mouth of *fools*.

The great God who formed everything gives the *fool* his hire and the transgressor his wages.

As a dog returns to his own vomit, so a *fool* repeats his *folly*.

Do you see a man wise in his own eyes? There is more hope for a *fool* than for him.

The Fool's Pay-Off

Why would anyone willingly choose the life of a fool? Why would anyone foolishly run down a path that leads to hardship, suffering and destruction? What's the upside, the advantage, the benefit, or the payoff for choosing to live and think like a fool?

Since most of our culture has embraced foolishness, what makes the life of a fool so deceptively appealing?

It's a problem of perspective and belief.

Our culture calls a "self-made man" a hero. We applaud the antics of someone who calls his own shots, who's a leader among leaders, who refuses to take "no" for an answer, and who cannot be deterred in his passionate quest for what he truly wants. We want to emulate the person who bows down to no one, who can "give better than he gets", and who is committed and single-focused on his own agenda and way of seeing things.

These are the attributes that create the celebrated icons of our society. These are the character traits that lead to success in this world. If you desire to live like your heroes, you will strive to duplicate their characteristics and values.

These are also the traits and convictions that make someone a fool in the eyes of Scripture. Just think about it. Our fallen, prideful culture says that the most important thing in this world is *me*. It's *my* wants, *my* rights, *my* desires, *my* opinions, *my* future, *my* calling, *my* happiness, *my* importance... *me, me, me*. The mantra goes: "If I can't love myself then I can't love others. I have to love me first." Or, as Shakespeare put it, "To thine own self be true."

To think and live like this makes you a fool in the eyes of the Lord.

The Heart of the Cross is Sacrifice

The heart of the Christian life, and the essence of the Christian message is love displayed in sacrifice and service to others. Jesus said "Greater love has no one than this, than to lay down one's life for his friends" (John 15:13).

If all this is true, why is the world almost irresistibly drawn to the lifestyle deemed as foolish by the Lord? Why can't they see the error of their ways, and the inevitable damning consequences of their selfish choices? Why is the world so blind to the truth and why do they not only reject, but literally detest, the "wisdom and instruction" of the Lord?

The answer is found in the cross of Christ.

The greatest act of self-sacrifice known to humanity was displayed by Christ on the cross, where He willingly died for the sins of others. This act of sacrifice and love is the agony of the ages. Nevertheless, it is considered by the lost, unregenerate world (those the Scripture calls fools) as *foolishness* to them. In other words, the world calls the cross of Christ "foolishness" and therefore becomes a "fool" by despising the "instruction and wisdom" of the Lord. What a tragic case of verbal gymnastics.

> **1 Corinthians 1:18** - For the *message* (preaching, power, wisdom and instruction)[3] of the cross is *foolishness* (moronic, absurdity, folly)[4] to (who) those who are *perishing* (the lost, the unredeemed, the world), but to *us* (the elect, the redeemed, the children of God) who are being saved it is the power of God.

But there's more.

> **1 Corinthians 1:19-31** - For it is written: "I will destroy the wisdom of the wise, and bring to nothing the understanding of the prudent." Where is the wise? Where is the scribe? Where is the disputer of this age? *Has not God made* (what) *foolish*

the wisdom of this world? For since, in the wisdom of God, the world through wisdom did not know God, it pleased God through the (what) foolishness of the message preached to save those who believe. For Jews request a sign, and Greeks seek after wisdom; but we preach Christ crucified, to the Jews a stumbling block and to the Greeks foolishness, but to those who are called, both Jews and Greeks, Christ the power of God and *the wisdom of God.* Because the *foolishness of God is wiser than men,* and the weakness of God is stronger than men. For you see your calling, brethren, that not many wise according to the flesh, not many mighty, not many noble, are called. *But God has chosen* (His action) *the foolish things of the world to put to shame the wise,* and God has chosen (His action) the weak things of the world to put to shame the things which are mighty; and the base things of the world and the things which are despised God has chosen (His action), and the things which are not, to bring to nothing the things that are, (why) that no flesh should glory in His presence. But of Him you are (what) *in Christ Jesus,* who became for us (1) *wisdom from God*—and (2) *righteousness* and (3) *sanctification* and (4) *redemption*— that, as it is written, "He who glories, let him glory in the LORD."

These words have eternal consequences. If you live in the world and believe this is the best life you can have right now, you will see the wisdom of God and the sacrifice of Christ as foolish or moronic. But if you live in the kingdom of God, you will understand that the "fear of the Lord is the beginning of knowledge, but fools" (those who reject the gospel and all it entails), by their very nature "despise wisdom and instruction" of the Lord (Prov. 1:7)

It's More than Mere Semantics

Which fool are you? Are you a *fool* in the eyes of the world for believing in the cross of Christ, or are you a *fool* in the eyes of Scripture who rejects the truths of God?

The consequences of your choice are eternal.

So choose wisely.

Getting Serious

1. Do you remember a time when you played the fool in order to gain the world and all it promised you? What was that like? Did the world deliver on its promises? Or were you left disappointed and empty-handed?

2. What was it like for you when you began to understand the cross of Christ for what it truly is? How did you pass from viewing it as mere foolishness to understanding and embracing it as the power and wisdom of God? (1 Cor. 1:18). Can you describe that experience? Have you had that experience?

3. Can you list a few examples from your own life when you despised the "knowledge and instruction" of the Lord? (Prov. 1:7). Are there things in His Word that you disagree with or refuse to accept and obey? If so, what are they? Do you see these instances as areas where you are despising God's knowledge and instruction? If so, does that make you a fool?

4. What changes are you committed to making in order to align your life with the eternal, infallible wisdom of God? Have you identified areas that need to change? Are you fervent enough in your faith to address those areas in your life, no matter the cost? If not, does that also make you a fool?

5. On a scale from 1 to 10, how would you rate God's wisdom in your life right now and in your decision making process? What was it yesterday? Are you growing in the wisdom of God? If not, why not?

Next Step Challenge

Using your Bible, look up the following verses in Proverbs that deal with the contrast between the wise man and the fool. Do a word study and define some of the terms used. Make sure you have a complete understanding of what the Lord is saying in these passages. Then ask yourself a few questions.

Proverbs 14:33 - Wisdom rests in the heart of him who has understanding, but what is in the heart of fools is made known.

Proverbs 17:16 - Why is there in the hand of a fool the purchase price of wisdom, since he has no heart for it?

Proverbs 18:2 - A fool has no delight in understanding, but in expressing his own heart.

What do these verses mean to you? Can you see yourself in any of these warnings and contrasts? If so, in what way? What does it mean when it says, "he has no heart for it" (Prov. 17:16)? Do you have a heart for God's wisdom?

What does it mean to be a fool today? Do you know anyone the Scriptures would deem a fool? Do you have any foolish traits in your own life? If so, what are you prepared to do about it?

Notes

1. Baker, W., & Carpenter, E. E. (2003). The complete word study dictionary: Old Testament (pp. 24–25). Chattanooga, TN: AMG Publishers.
2. Ibid., 122-123.
3. Zodhiates, S. (2000). The complete word study dictionary: New Testament (pp. 925-926). Chattanooga, TN: AMG Publishers.
4. Ibid., 1001.

DAY THIRTEEN

The Lost Art of Listening

My son, hear the instruction of your father,
and do not forsake the law of your mother.
Proverbs 1:8

W E LIVE IN A WORLD that was birthed in the bed of rebellion. From Eve's rebellion in the Garden of Eden to the murder of Abel by his brother Cain, we see the sin of rebellion. The open, hostile rejection of authority is one of the bedrocks of human existence.

Rebellion's beginning is far older than the book of Genesis. It was rebellion that caused the Lord to banish Satan and his followers from heaven and cast them down to the earth (Isaiah 14:13-15). That's why Satan is known as the "god of this age" (2 Cor. 4:4) and the "prince of the power of the air" (Eph. 2:2). Satan even boasted of this when he tried to tempt Jesus by offering to give Him "all the kingdoms of the world" if He would just "worship before me" (Luke 4:5-7).

What's at the root of all rebellion? Pride.

It was pride that brought mighty King Nebuchadnezzar low and drove him out into the fields, living on all fours and eating grass like a humbled animal (Dan. 4:33). It was pride that led Pharaoh to vainly fight against the Lord and not only see the destruction of all Egypt, but of his own house and family. It was pride that almost kept Naaman from being healed of leprosy (2 Kings 5:11), and pride that saw Haman hanged on the gallows he prepared for Mordecai (Esther 7:10). It was the sin of pride that foolishly led Peter to proclaim his commitment to Jesus as greater than the other disciples when he said, "Even if all are made to stumble, yet I will not be" (Mark 14:29).

The Lord says He hates "pride and arrogance and the evil way" (Prov. 8:13) and that the prideful are so enamored with themselves they do not "seek God." Nor is God in any of their thoughts (Psalm 10:4). They are clueless, self-deceived, and so inwardly-focused that they can see nothing but themselves. They have become the center of their self-created universe, and the most valued and important thing in their lives. Their personal happiness and pleasure is the all-consuming passion of their short, sad lives. The Lord promises to humble the man who exalts himself (Matt. 23:12) and to bring to nothing the one who arrogantly smirks at both God and others (Isaiah 2:11).

The future of the proud and rebellious is indeed bleak.

Rebellion and Our DNA

We are a people that see pride and rebellion as one of the core values of our society. We spend countless hours watching movies and sitcoms that are saturated with the theme of pride. Our popular music exalts self to the point that we've elevated self-indulgence and narcissism to an art form. Even in some churches, the worship leader (our own version of a personal Christian rock star) gets more face time and notoriety than the Lord Jesus.

We, as a people, rebel against anything and everything. Rebellion is both cool and popular. Pride, which is the source of our rebellion, is deemed a virtue in our culture. Just think, we rebel against our government and refuse to be "subject to the governing authorities" as commanded in Scripture (Rom. 13:1-4). Our nation was founded on rebellion and we wear that rebellion as a badge of honor and celebrate it each July 4th as a national holiday. We rebel against our employers, miserly giving as little as possible, yet demanding they pay us all the more, always grumbling and never content with our wages. We do this in direct contradiction to the Word of God (Col. 3:22-25). We rebel against the authorities placed over us for our own good, such as teachers, law enforcement personnel, older siblings, pastors and ministers.

Most importantly, we rebel against our parents, or any person who lovingly dares to place expectations or standards upon us that we disagree with, or which stifle our drive for independence. Rebellion begins almost as soon as we learn to walk.

In our culture, parents are portrayed as "out of touch old fogies", "old fashioned geezers", or "ignorant killjoys" that won't let their children do whatever they want to do. The children are often seen as the ones who have it all together; the ones who think rationally and have their emotions in check; the ones who see the big picture without getting sidetracked by issues involving respect, obedience, diligence, commitment, honesty and hard work.

The last thing our children want to do today is ask their parents for advice or follow their instructions. Yet that's the exact admonition the Lord gives us in Proverbs.

Learning How to Listen and Obey

Consider the words from a loving father to his naive, impressionable son:

> **Proverbs 1:8** - My son, hear the instruction of your father, and do not forsake the law of your mother.

In this proverb we find the father, as head of his home and family, imploring his young son to listen and hear the law and wisdom of his parents. The father wants to protect his son from the evil, hurtful things in this world that will ruin the young man's life. We know this because all good fathers want to keep their children from stepping on the same land mines they did. All good fathers want to protect their children from suffering the same hurts or making the same mistakes they did when they were young, simple-minded, and thought they knew everything.

So here we have the father speaking to his son, to "My son"— and pleading with him to "hear the instruction of your father" and not "forsake the law of your mother" (Prov. 1:8). This plea is not generic, but a deeply personal and passionate plea coming from the lips of a loving father to his naive, gullible young son. In fact, the phrase "My son" is used almost twenty times in the book of Proverbs.[1]

What's at the core of the plea? To "hear" or "listen" to someone wiser than yourself.

The word translated "hear" is *shama* in the Hebrew and means more than just letting sounds bounce off your ear drums to cause a recognizable vibration. It means to "listen" or "hearken" and then to "obey" what has been heard.[2] It's a two-fold definition. It means to both *listen* and *obey*. Not one or the other.

To "listen and obey" what? The "*instruction* (discipline, chastening, and correction, with the imagery of a father disciplining his son that he loves)[3] of your father." The command is to "listen and obey" what the father has to say. The word for *instruction* is the same word we find in Proverbs 1:2, 3, 7. It's the same *instruction* that "fools despise" in Proverbs 1:7. It's the same *instruction* God promised to reveal in the book of Proverbs (Prov. 1:2). And it's the same *instruction* given us by the indwelling of the Holy Spirit.

But listening without obedience is still disobedience. For the son to listen to the instruction of the father and not obey that instruction is the same as not listening at all. It's nothing more than pride and rebellion and a forsaking of the "law of your mother" (Prov. 1:8).

To Forsake is to Abandon

The word "forsake" means to "leave alone, ignore, or abandon."[4] The Hebrew word for "law" is *torah* and is a general term for "instruction and direction", either from God or man.[5] The command is to listen and obey the instruction and discipline of your father and to not ignore or forsake the directions of your mother. Both parents are important. Both are involved in shaping the character of the young man.

The son's only job in all of this is to not be a fool. Instead, he is to "listen and obey" the words of the two people who've loved him more than anyone else on the face of the earth. He's to embrace and not forsake the directions given to him by his parents— the ones who have sacrificed their lives to give him life and a future. Part of their instruction is to impart the wisdom they have accumulated over the years, after making many of the same mistakes they're hoping to keep their son from repeating.

It's classic Parenting 101.

The Lost Art of Listening

One of the great tragedies facing the young son is this: There is so much noise surrounding him that it makes it difficult, if not impossible, for him to hear the needed words of wisdom. It's the same for us today. Everywhere we go we're surrounded by noise. The radio is constantly playing in the car, even when we're not consciously listening to it. It's a natural force of habit when we drive. We have the sound of the television playing in the background, even when we're not watching and don't know what's on. It's always there. Just a constant hum of music and dialogue. When we walk, run, sit, or wait in line, we instinctively cram in our earbuds. We try to drown out the sounds of reality with the noise of our own choosing— as if the latest song is more important than the people and activities of life all around us.

Listening and hearing are rapidly becoming a lost art and the consequences for the church and the Christian are catastrophic. Consider the importance of being able to hear, listen to, and ultimately obey the Word of God:

> **Proverbs 2:1-2, 5** - My son, if you receive my words, and treasure my commands within you, so that you *incline your ear* to wisdom (to listen and

hear), and *apply your heart* to understanding (to obey)... then you will understand the fear of the Lord, and find the knowledge of God.

Romans 10:17 - So then faith comes by *hearing*, and *hearing* by the word of God.

John 10:27-28 - "My sheep *hear* My voice, and I know them, and they follow Me. And I give them eternal life, and they shall never perish; neither shall anyone snatch them out of My hand."

What does this say about those who don't hear His voice? What if our lives are so filled with the noise and chaos of this life that the voice of Jesus is being drowned out?

Over and over again we find this admonition from the Lord Jesus, in both the gospels and the book of Revelation:

"He who has an ear to *hear*, let him *hear*!"[6]

The Lord is not One who is loud, brash, boisterous or pushy, demanding to be heard. He's actually quite the opposite. After the Mount Carmel experience, He revealed Himself to Elijah at the mouth of a cave. He could have revealed Himself in the "great and strong wind" that "tore into the mountains and broke the rocks in pieces" (1 Kings 19:11). But He didn't. Nor was He found in the mighty "earthquake" or the consuming "fire" that passed in front of Elijah. Instead, the Lord used a "still small voice" (1 Kings 19:12) that refused to compete with any of these things. It was a voice so small and so still that you could easily miss it if you weren't listening closely.

If we will take the time to shut out the noise of the temporal and listen intently to the voice of the eternal, the voice that Elijah heard will speak to us today.

When we hear the Lord's voice unmistakably breaking through the noise and clatter of our lives, our only response is to obey. We must listen and obey, just like the wise and loving father implored his young son to do.

> **Proverbs 1:8** - My son, hear the instruction of your father, and do not forsake the law of your mother.

Because nothing else really matters.

Getting Serious

1. Has God ever spoken to you? If so, what was it like? How did it happen? What did God tell you when He spoke into your life? What have you done in response to that event?
2. Has God ever convicted you of something in your life that you've refused to change, correct or surrender to Him? If so, what was it? How did He communicate His will to you and why have you refused to obey Him?
3. Are there areas in your life that reek of rebellion? Are there areas that you have defiantly refused to give over to Him? What are you waiting for? Do you view your disobedience in much softer, generic, politically correct terms than rebellion? Does the terminology you use make your rebellion less of a sin?
4. Do you obey your parents in all things? How about your husband, your employer, or the government? How do you view the authority of the church, your pastor, elders and ministers? Do you love your wife as Christ loved the church?[7] Is the Lord trying to speak to you in any of these areas?
5. On a scale from 1 to 10, how would you rate God's wisdom in your life right now and in your decision making process? What was it yesterday? Are you growing in the wisdom of God? If not, why not?

Next Step Challenge

Using your Bible, look up the phrase "He who has an ear, let Him hear." You will find it in the following verses.

Matthew 11:15; 13:9, 43
Mark 4:9, 23; 7:16
Luke 8:8, 14:35
Revelation 2:7, 11, 17, 29; 3:6, 13, 22

Read the phrase in context to determine what Jesus was speaking about when He made this all-important, yet somewhat cryptic statement.

What does "He who has an ear, let him hear" really mean? Was Jesus speaking to everyone? If not, who was He speaking to and what was He saying to them? What was He trying to emphasize? Can you see a pattern in any of this? If so, what is the pattern?

What does it mean for you today? Do you have "ears to hear"? Are you listening? If so, what is He saying and what are you prepared to do about it?

Notes

1. Proverbs 1:8, 10, 15; 2:1; 3:1, 11, 4:10, 20, 5:1, 5:20; 6:1, 20; 7:1; 19:27; 23:15, 19, 26; 24:13, 21; 27:11; 31:2.
2. Baker, W., & Carpenter, E. E. (2003). The complete word study dictionary: Old Testament (pp. 1166-1167). Chattanooga, TN: AMG Publishers.
3. Ibid., 582.
4. Ibid., 729.
5. Ibid., 1220.
6. Matthew 11:15; 13:9, 43; Mark 4:9, 23; 7:16; Luke 8:8, 14:35; Revelation 2:7, 11, 17, 29; 3:6, 13, 22.
7. Ephesians 5:25

DAY FOURTEEN

No Equality in Heaven

For they will be a graceful ornament on your head,
and chains about your neck.

Proverbs 1:9

W E LIVE IN A TIME WHEN PEOPLE fight for equal
rights: The right to vote, the right to work, the right to say
what we want, the right to marry who we want, the right to do
what we want, the right to live, and the right to die. It seems like
we all want to be equal in our own eyes and with everybody else,
with no one standing out among the crowd and no one having
more than another.

This drive for equality has now invaded almost every facet of
our lives. We don't give trophies to the winners in Little League
Baseball anymore, because everyone must be equal. There are no
winners and no losers. Everyone gets a trophy for just
participating, for simply showing up, or for buying a glove and a

pair of cleats. By not honoring the winners (the ones who deserve the honor and who earned the recognition) it's somehow supposed to make us all feel special. We're all striving for equality, which always tends to settle at the lowest common denominator.

That's not how life functions in the real world. It's the best and brightest, the ones who work the hardest, the ones who put in the long hours, and the ones who continually strive to learn more who get rewarded. They are the ones with the raise, the promotion, the starting position, or the corner office. It's not the lazy, half-hearted sluggard who's honored in our society. The rewards and accolades go to the few who work diligently, and not to the many who don't.

As sobering as it might sound, the Kingdom of Heaven functions in much the same way.

The Rewards for Obedience

The father and mother in this proverb have implored their young son to stay the course and keep focused on the things in life that really matter. They know that he is about to enter into the fallen world of sin, deceit and deception. Thus, they are giving him their final words of affirmation to keep him strong, no matter what he might face.

The father tells him: "My son, *hear* (listen and obey) the *instruction* (discipline, correction, chastening)[1] of your father, and do not *forsake* (abandon, walk away from, ignore)[2] the *law* (direction) of your mother" (Prov. 1:8). In other words, remember how we've raised you. Remember what you've been taught. Remember the truth and do not walk away from it, chasing other idols the world will try to tempt you with.

Remember and stay strong.

Why should the son listen to the "instruction" of his father and follow the "law" of his mother? What will he gain from placing himself in a position that is sure to bring about ridicule and rejection from his peers? What's the pay-off for this young man? What's the upside to living a sin-free, committed life in Christ?

> **Proverbs 1:9** - For *they* (the "instruction of your father" and the "law of your mother") will be a *graceful ornament* (a garland, wreath, a decorative headpiece worn as a sign of approval, honor, favor and acceptance)[3] *on your head* (as a crown), and *chains about your neck* (a necklace of remembrance).

The graceful ornament symbolizes wisdom and prosperity coming from the father to the son and is his for the asking, if he obeys. It is the son's reward for listening, heeding and obeying the words of his father.

This leads to a few questions and conclusions about rewards.

We are not talking about salvation. The payment for the penalty of our sins is a free gift. We could never do enough to earn salvation. Salvation is based on our faith in the completed work of Christ on the cross. Therefore, salvation is not a reward (Rom. 6:23; Eph. 2:8-9).

All of us are equally in need of forgiveness and grace at the foot of the cross. We are simply one hopeless beggar telling another beggar where we found bread.

What we are talking about are the rewards that will be given by Christ, based on what we have done with the precious and costly gift of salvation. The rewards will be given according to how faithful we have been to Him while living on this side of eternity. In regards to this, we can surmise the following:

One, the reward is conditional. If the son listens and obeys, the reward is his. If he does not listen and obey, does he still receive the reward for just participating, for simply being a member of the family, or being on the team? The context would say, "No."

Two, the reward is for him alone. Nowhere is the promise given to the lost and disobedient, or to those who are not the father's child. Does this mean that not everyone is entitled to the reward? Is it exclusively reserved for some, but not all, and given only to the ones who meet the requirements of obedience? The context would say, "Yes."

Three, equality is not the issue. The reward makes the son special in the eyes of the father. It's a recognition of his grace, favor, love and acceptance of the son, based on the son's faithful adherence to the instructions of the father. Does this mean not everyone is equal in the eyes of the father? Does it mean that there will be some who receive rewards while others do not? If this is true, is the granting of rewards primarily based, as in this verse, on obedience to the father? Again, the context would say, "Yes."

The Stephanos

In the New Testament we discover there are five crowns that the believer can receive. The operative word is *can*. These crowns are not guaranteed for just showing up. In fact, the Greek word used for "crown" is *stephanos* and doesn't refer to a kingly crown, as a monarch would wear, but a "crown or wreath or garland that was given to the victor in the public games."[4] This is more of an overcoming crown given to those who have trained, fought well and won. In Scripture we find what is called the "imperishable crown" (1 Cor. 9:24-25). Next, there is the "crown of rejoicing" (1 Thess. 2:19). Then, the "crown of righteousness" (2 Tim. 4:8), the "crown of glory" (1 Peter 5:4), and finally the "crown of life" (James 1:12 and Rev. 2:10).

Again, these crowns are not guaranteed for just participating. They are given to those who have met some sort of requirement. They are rewarded to those who have distinguished themselves among others. They are not for everyone. They are only for the few who have earned them.

For example:

> **1 Corinthians 9:24** - Do you not know that those who run in a race all run, but *one receives the prize?* Run in such a way that you may obtain it.

This verse implies that there are some who will not run the race heartily and will not obtain the prize or crown. The admonition is for you to be different, to not be like the crowd, and to run to win.

> **2 Timothy 4:8** - Finally, there is laid up for me the crown of righteousness, which the Lord, the righteous Judge, will give to me on that Day, and not to me only but also to *all who have loved His appearing.*

What if you don't love the reality of His appearing? What if you're so enamored with this world you are of no good to the kingdom? What if you love this world (1 John 2:15) and not the certainty of His appearing? Do you still qualify for the crown?

> **James 1:12** - Blessed is the man who *endures temptation*; for when *he has been approved*, he will receive the crown of life which the Lord has promised to those who love Him.

What if you do not endure temptation? What happens then? Are you still given the crown? Or have you, by your own actions, disqualified yourself for the prize (the promised crown) by not meeting the requirements? To be exact, what is the requirement for approval? Is it simply our love for Him? If so, how is our love for Him manifested daily to make us approved or accepted in Him?

Casting Crowns

Many of us who have been brought up in the "everyone is equal, so there's no need to try too hard" morass of our fallen culture have come to believe that working for crowns or rewards is a futile effort, since we don't get to keep them anyway. After all, Revelation 4:10-11 shows the twenty-four elders— who represent the church, the redeemed, you and me—"casting their crowns before the throne" in a profound act of worship.

We then reason, "If I'm going to cast my crown that I've worked so hard for at the feet of Jesus, what's the point? I'll be just like everyone else who doesn't have a crown. So why try? Why should I work for a reward that I can't keep? It seems like a big waste of time to me."

A response like that only shows the depravity of our love and commitment to our Lord. We give Him the glory with our lips, as long as we can keep the rewards to make us feel special and important among our friends. How selfish is that?

Do not be deceived. Salvation is a gift given freely by grace through the sacrifice of our Lord Jesus. In this, we are all equal. What we do with the gift (how we live our lives in Christ and for His glory) is another matter indeed. The Scriptures have much to say about how truly unequal we will be in His kingdom.

> **Matthew 5:12** - "Rejoice and be exceedingly glad, (why) for *great is your reward in heaven*, for so they persecuted the prophets who were before you."

"Great" is a relative term. Great is only great when compared to something less than great. Those who are persecuted for the name of Christ will have a "great" reward in heaven, compared to other rewards, or compared to those who receive no rewards. In other words, their reward will be greater than others. Otherwise, why are we given the admonition to be "exceedingly glad" in the face of horrific persecution and even death?

> **1 Corinthians 3:14** - If anyone's work which he has built on it (what) *endures*, he will receive a reward.

And if it doesn't endure? Exactly.

> **Matthew 16:27** - "For the Son of Man will come in the glory of His Father with His angels, and then He will *reward each* (how) *according to his works*."

The reward is applied "according to his works" in differing degrees, based on differing degrees of works, just like it is in the real world. Jesus rewards the faithful steward of ten coins with having "authority over ten cities" and the faithful steward with five coins of having "authority over five cities." Yet the unfaithful steward entrusted with one coin receives nothing (Luke 19:15-26). Jesus went so far as to reward the steward with ten coins even more by giving him the one coin from the unfaithful servant. Was that unfair? Was Jesus playing favorites? What about the faithful steward who was given five coins? Was there something wrong with him? Or was Jesus simply rewarding the most faithful with more?

So it is with you and me in His kingdom.

Jesus is Coming Soon

Jesus is coming soon and He is bringing His rewards with Him. He says so in Revelation 22:12: "And behold, I am coming quickly, and My reward is with Me, to give to (who) *every one* (how) *according to his work.*"

What does "everyone according to his work" mean?

To those who "hear", and are faithful to listen and obey "the instruction of your father" and not "forsake the law of your mother" (Prov. 1:8), the reward for obedience will be a "graceful ornament on your head, and chains about your neck" (Prov. 1:9). Our Lord is a "rewarder of those who *diligently* seek Him" (Heb. 11:6). He rewards the diligent, the committed, the single-focused, the sold-out, the passionate, the faithful, the devoted, and those that seek Him "as the deer pants for the water brooks, so pants my soul for You, O God" (Psalm 42:1). But He never promises to reward the slacker, the half-hearted, the lazy, the slothful, the indifferent, or the apathetic. Never. And neither would you.

Those who put heaven first and this life last will see great reward. Those who don't will suffer shame.

As C.S Lewis said in *Mere Christianity*, "If you read history, you will find that Christians who did most for the present world were just those who thought most of the next. Aim at Heaven and you will get earth thrown in. Aim at earth and you will get neither."

Let's strive to be so heavenly minded that we are of no earthly good.

Getting Serious

1. What are you committed to? What's the driving passion of your life? Be honest with yourself. You don't have to give the Sunday School answer. Do you know what you're committed to? If so, how do you know?

2. How much time do you spend on what you're committed to? How much of your life is tied up in this pursuit? Can others see your commitment? Are you known to others by your commitment? How have your passions impacted other areas of your life?

3. Have you received any rewards for your passions? Have you received any notoriety or recognition because of what you're committed to? How did it make you feel? Was the feeling lasting? Was the end result worth the time you spent to get the special recognition?

4. Have you thought about how temporal and short-lived all the things we're committed to in this world truly are, either good or bad? Our commitments often involve our jobs, our degrees, money, fame, a good-looking physique, a new car, stylish clothes, a fat retirement account, a second or third vacation home, etc. Even if these things are noble causes, like ending world hunger or bringing about world peace, they will eventually pass away. Have you considered the fact that the only wise thing to commit your life to is the reality of the next world, the eternal world, and your life in Christ? If so, what are you waiting for?

5. On a scale from 1 to 10, how would you rate God's wisdom in your life right now and in your decision making process? What was it yesterday? Are you growing in the wisdom of God? If not, why not?

Next Step Challenge

Using your Bible, look up the five crowns listed in the New Testament and read about them in context. You will find them in the verses below.

1 Corinthians 9:24-25
1 Thessalonians 2:19
2 Timothy 4:8
1 Peter 5:4
James 1:12 and **Revelation 2:10**

What are these verses saying? Can you obtain the five crowns for yourself? What would you have to do or not do to meet the requirements for each crown? Are you interested? Does it seem like something to commit time and serious thought to?

What is more important to you than receiving a reward from the Lord Jesus and joyously, as an act of worship, giving it back to Him? Won't you feel embarrassed to have nothing to cast at His feet?

If so, what are you prepared to do about it?

Notes

1. Baker, W., & Carpenter, E. E. (2003). The complete word study dictionary: Old Testament (p. 582). Chattanooga, TN: AMG Publishers.
2. Ibid., 729.
3. Ibid., 545.
4. Zodhiates, S. (2000). The complete word study dictionary: New Testament. (pp. 1311-1312). Chattanooga, TN: AMG Publishers.

DAY FIFTEEN

The Quick Slide into Sin

My son, if sinners entice you,
Do not consent.
Proverbs 1:10

BEFORE WE DIG ANY DEEPER into the next section of Proverbs, let's pause for a moment and take an aerial overview of the next twelve verses. We can begin the process by looking at one of the most overlooked and ignored warnings in all of Scripture: 1 Corinthians 15:33.

Here the Lord tells us to not be deceived.

But what should we not be deceived about?

> **1 Corinthians 15:33** - Do not be deceived: "Evil company corrupts good habits."

What exactly do "evil company" and "good habits" mean? And what do they have to do with Proverbs? Let's find the answers.

First, what it says:

> **1 Corinthians 15:33** - Do not be *deceived* (to be led astray, to wander, to roam aimlessly, to be led away from the truth and into error and sin, to mislead, to seduce)[1]: "*Evil* (bad, worthless, wicked, vicious, malicious, cowardly, destructive)[2] *company* (companionship, communion, conversation, speech, talk)[3] *corrupts* (destroys, spoils, waste away, to utterly decay, to corrupt fully, to deprave)[4] *good* (moral, useful, pleasing, virtuous)[5] *habits* (morals, character, one's manner of life)[6]."

Then, what it means:

The Lord is warning us to not be easily deceived into thinking His Words and admonitions are meant for someone else, and not for us. Maybe He meant them for someone not quite as spiritual as we are, someone not quite as mature, or someone not quite as smart. Maybe they are for someone weaker, someone more naive, or someone who can't be trusted to always do the right thing at the right time, like we can.

It's that kind of thinking that gets us into trouble every time.

The Warnings

The first warning is about deception. We're not to be deceived into thinking what God is telling us is either not true, or doesn't apply in our situation. We're not to be deceived into believing this warning was meant for someone else. Tragically, that's exactly the rationalization each of us makes regarding God's Word. Whenever His Word will not allow us to do what we want to do and what we think is right, we rationalize. We want to follow our heart, and to our own self be true. Yet we willingly forget that God says our heart is "deceitful above all things and desperately wicked" (Jer. 17:9). In order to have the knowledge of God, our heart is the very last thing we should want to follow.

But we still follow our heart over and over again.

We never seem to learn.

The second warning is about the root of the deception. It's the lie that we can play with fire and not get burned. We can roll around in the mud with the farm animals and not get dirty. We can live like the world, think like the world, look like the world, value what the world values, crave the world's love and acceptance, and still remain pure from the world. How stupid is that?

God tells us there is a one-way path when we associate with evil people. Just one way. The way leads from purity to defilement, from virtue to sin, from light to darkness, and from worth and value to corruption and decay. It's a one way street that leads from holiness to depravity, and not the other way around.

"But I know the Jesus in me will change their hearts if I just spend enough time with them and do the things they are doing." Don't be deceived.

"But I love him! I know if we date or get married he will someday see the Jesus in me and become a Christian. I just know it!" You're being deceived.

"Hey, they're my friends. I can hang with them and just not do what they are doing. You know, I can be a light in their darkness." You're deceived.

Non-believers never become believers by osmosis. That takes a sovereign act of God. You've been warned by the Lord not to be deceived into thinking good morals or good character will redeem bad company. The truth is just the opposite. Don't be deceived into thinking this warning from God doesn't apply in your case, for whatever reason you conjure up in your mind to justify your disobedience.

It's not going to happen, because God doesn't lie.

The Addiction to Peer Pressure

We see this scenario graphically played out for us in a young man's life throughout the first chapter of Proverbs. It's peer pressure run amuck. It's the "us" and "we" and "they" and "everyone" against the "you" and "your" and the faithfulness of God's Word. It's a picture of the temptation of peer pressure—and of classic failure.

Notice, if you will, the gracious warning from the father and mother and the corresponding blessings that come from heeding the same warning.

> **Proverbs 1:8** - My son, hear the instruction of your father, and do not forsake the law of your mother; (why) for they (the instruction and the law) will be a graceful ornament on your head, and chains about your neck.

Again, **Proverbs 1:8** - My son, *hear* (listen, obey, proclaim to others)[7] the *instruction* (correction, discipline)[8] of your father, and do not *forsake* (abandon, cast off or away, to leave alone)[9] the *law* (direction, custom, manner of living)[10] of your mother; (why) for *they* (the instruction and discipline of your father and the law or custom or manner of living or example of your mother) will be a *graceful ornament on your head* (a wreath of grace, a garland), and *chains about your neck*.

The phrase "a graceful ornament" seems strange to our ears today. What is it exactly? It's a garland, a wreath, or a decorative headpiece worn as a sign of approval and honor and is given as a result of following wisdom.[11] It's actually awarded by wisdom herself (Prov. 4:9).

The "chains about your neck" might give us the mental picture of Mr. T,[12] or of a rap artist with a wad of bling hanging from his neck. That's not what this passage is talking about. It's a necklace, and is used figuratively of wearing a parent's instructions around one's neck as a valued chain of remembrance.

In other words, do not forsake what you've been taught. Do not abandon the acceptance and honor you've already received by not living a life of wisdom. Do not throw it all away for the fleeting approval of the world. Do not become friends with those the Lord commands otherwise. And do not make yourself an enemy of God.

James 4:4 - Adulterers and adulteresses! Do you not know that friendship with the world is *enmity* (hostility, hatred, enemy)[13] with God? Whoever therefore *wants* (desires, is inclined)[14] to be a friend of the world *makes himself an enemy of God.*

Who in their right mind would want to make themselves an enemy of God? But that's exactly what happens when we desire the friendship of the world. Hence, "Do not be deceived: Evil company corrupts good habits" (1 Cor. 15:33).

The Quick Slide into Sin

The most frightening part of this entire section is how quickly temptation comes upon the young son, regardless of the warnings of the loving father. The temptation comes to him, just like it comes to each of us, at the level of our personal felt needs. In other words, we are tempted in the area of our perceived incompleteness in life, where we feel God somehow shortchanged us and didn't supply all we needed to *feel* loved, secure, cherished, accepted or important. Therefore, we think we have to fill those "felt needs" by ourselves, in our own fallen ways, through any means possible.

We all know what that looks like.

If someone makes us *feel* insecure because of their inherent popularity, charisma or charm, we are tempted to trash and degrade them in our minds, or with our words, in order to make ourselves *feel* better by comparison (as if tearing them down will somehow automatically raise us up in the eyes of others, and make us *feel* better about ourselves). This sort of thing doesn't change anything about us, and it certainly doesn't change anything about them. We're just trying to convince ourselves that our light is shining brighter now because we've worked so hard to try to dim their light.

If we feel lonely, empty and worthless because everyone else has a significant other and we don't, we're tempted to lower our standards and settle for whoever we can get, even if we know that "evil company corrupts good habits", character and morals (1 Cor. 15:33). We're even willing to be deceived in that area as long as our felt needs are met and we begin to *feel* better about ourselves. Our own personal needs, our inward view of ourselves, and the way we *feel* about the person staring back at us in the mirror often trumps the truth of God. Like spoiled children, we want our "cake" and "we want to eat it too", regardless of what the Word of God says.

That's why seemingly good kids join gangs. That's why church kids become sexually active. That's why the divorce rate among professing Christians is just as high as among the lost (the ones devoid of the Holy Spirit, and the same ones we are trying to lead to Christ). Indeed, that's why the pull of the world and the draw of our own flesh— our desires, emotions and feelings of self-worth— are the hotbed of most of the temptations we face.

That's also why we so easily fall into temptation in those areas.

All for One and One for All!

We're going to see just how quickly temptation can come to the young son in this proverb, and how utterly appealing it all sounds— especially when peer pressure is added to the mix.

It's just like the motto of the Three Musketeers: "All for One and One for All!"

That's the next topic we'll look at.

Getting Serious

1. What kind of temptations do you face on a daily basis? Are they primarily centered in areas outside of yourself, such as drugs, sex, theft, etc.? Or are they primarily centered in areas within yourself, such as anger, fear, lust, unforgiveness, insecurity and gossip?

2. How do you deal with the temptations centered outside of yourself? How do you deal with the ones centered within yourself? Do you deal with them the same or differently?

3. Where are you in your walk with Christ? Are you drawing closer to Him each day? Are there areas in your life He has spoken to you about, yet you have refused to repent, change, and walk away from them? If there are those areas, why haven't you dealt with them before now? Are you afraid? Weak? Ignorant? What is it exactly?

4. Do you have people in your life that 1 Corinthians 15:33 would speak to? Are there relationships that have the possibility of corrupting your character and morals? If so, what are you prepared to do about them? Be honest with yourself. Are you currently being deceived in the area of your friends?

5. On a scale from 1 to 10, how would you rate God's wisdom in your life right now and in your decision making process? What was it yesterday? Are you growing in the wisdom of God? If not, why not?

Next Step Challenge

In the Sermon on the Mount, Jesus took the Law (which basically governed overt behaviors, or the sinful act itself) and made it a matter of the heart. He said, for example,

Outward Behavior:
"You have heard that it was said to those of old, 'You shall not murder' (overt sinful act), and whoever murders will be in danger of the judgment."

Inward Motivation:
"But I say to you that whoever is angry with his brother without a cause shall be in danger of the judgment. And whoever says to his brother, 'Raca!' shall be in danger of the council. But whoever says, 'You fool!' shall be in danger of hell fire" (Matt. 5:21-22).

As you can see, Jesus went from the symptom, "murder" to the cause, "anger". In doing so, He began to speak about a man's inward passions (his own felt needs).

While using your Bible, write down all the times in the Sermon on the Mount (Matthew 5-7) where Jesus went from a symptom to a cause. Notice what He said about adultery, unforgivness, pride, etc. Once you've written them all down, pray and ask the Lord to speak to you in your own life about what you've just learned.

Ask Him to give you wisdom regarding the temptation to sin.

Note:

1. Zodhiates, S. (2000). The complete word study dictionary: New Testament. (p. 1166). Chattanooga, TN: AMG Publishers.
2. Ibid., 809-810.
3. Ibid., 1039.
4. Ibid., 1442-1443.
5. Ibid., 1492.
6. Ibid., 708-709.
7. Ibid., 1166-1167.
8. Ibid., 582.
9. Ibid., 729.
10. Ibid., 1220.
11. Ibid., 545.
12. Mr. T (Lawrence Tureaud) is an American actor who is easily recognized by his trademark gold jewelry, African Mandinka hairstyle, and his tough guy persona. He played boxer Clubber Lange in the 1982 classic film, Rocky III (my favorite in the Rocky franchise).
13. Zodhiates, S. (2000). The complete word study dictionary: New Testament (p. 692). Chattanooga, TN: AMG Publishers.
14. Ibid., 347.

DAY SIXTEEN

Our Addiction to Peer Pressure

My son, if sinners entice you,
Do not consent.
Proverbs 1:10

ONE OF THE MOST OVERLOOKED and ignored warnings in all of Scripture is found in 1 Corinthians 15:33. Here the Lord tells us not to be deceived about something we think we're immune to. He is referring to peer pressure.

> **1 Corinthians 15:33** - Do not be deceived: "Evil company corrupts good habits."

Or, to expand the verse a bit:

> **1 Corinthians 15:33** - Do not be *deceived* (to be led astray, to wander, to roam aimlessly, to be led away

from the truth and into error and sin, to mislead, to seduce):[1] "*Evil* (bad, worthless, wicked, vicious, malicious, cowardly, destructive)[2] *company* (companionship, communion, conversation, speech, talk)[3] *corrupts* (destroys, spoils, waste away, to utterly decay, to corrupt fully, to deprave)[4] *good* (moral, useful, pleasing, virtuous)[5] *habits* (morals, character, one's manner of life)."[6]

The Lord is warning us to not be easily deceived into thinking His Words don't apply to us at this time, as though they're meant for someone else. Maybe we'll admit that they could apply to us at some point in our life. But not today, and certainly not in this relationship.

As usual, this kind of mental rationalization gets us into trouble every time, just as the loving father feared would happen to his young son.

The Quick Slide into Sin and Judgment

At almost the speed of light, watch how quickly temptation can come to this young son and entice him into sin. Pay careful attention to the detail in which the father warns his loved, naive, gullible son about the ways of the world and the temptations he will face.

> **Proverbs 1:10** - My son, *if* (when) *sinners* (those reckoned as offenders, those facing condemnation for their actions, those under the wrath and judgment of God)[7] *entice* (deceive, persuade, allure)[8]

you, (what) *do not consent* (yield, be willing, acquiesces).[9]

There's the ever present appeal to the flesh— the almost irresistible compulsion for acceptance, power, anticipation, greed, lust, companionship and belonging. All of what is to be found in Christ is used as a temptation to entice the young son away from Christ and into a life of sin.

Have you ever been there? Does any of this sound familiar?

Do we not sin to satisfy, in our selfish flesh and in our own ways, the same needs Christ promised to fulfill for us in His own flesh?

Take a look at where these temptations hit the young son and what needs he tries to fulfill apart from Christ.

Acceptance and Belonging

> **Proverbs 1:11a** - *If* (when) they say, "*Come with us* (acceptance and belonging)…"

Power, Violence and Excitement

> **Proverbs 1:11b-12** - "Let *us* (acceptance and belonging) *lie in wait* (excitement) to *shed blood* (power and violence); let *us* (acceptance and belonging) *lurk secretly* (excitement) for the *innocent without cause* (power and violence); let *us* (acceptance and belonging) s*wallow them alive like Sheol* (power), and whole, *like those who go down to the Pit* (power)."

Greed, Lust and the Love of Money

> **Proverbs 1:13** - "*We* (acceptance and belonging) shall find all kinds of *precious possessions* (greed, lust and the love of money), *we* (acceptance and belonging) shall *fill our houses with spoil* (greed, lust and the love of money)."

Companionship and Belonging

> **Proverbs 1:14** - "Cast in your lot among *us* (companionship and belonging), let *us* (acceptance and belonging) *all have one purse* (companionship)."

The Warning from Our Father

The father (our Father) reveals to his son (you and me) the end result of a life lived in the flesh. It's the natural consequence of being deceived about "evil company" (1 Cor. 15:33). First, he gives the stern warning to not even get close to those under the wrath of God. Don't even associate with them or "walk in the way with them" he says. We are not to be bound or yoked together by friendship or affection with unbelievers. "Do not be unequally yoked together with unbelievers. For what fellowship has righteousness with lawlessness? And what communion has light with darkness" (2 Cor. 6:14)?

> **Proverbs 1:15** - My son, *do not walk in the way with them* (in their manner or course of life, on their journey), *keep your foot from* (what) *their path.*

This reminds us of the importance of staying completely free from the contaminating influence of the world, the ungodly, the sinful, and the scornful, and to have as our delight the things of God— even His law and His decrees.

> **Psalm 1:1-2** - Blessed is the man who (what) *walks not in the counsel of the ungodly*, nor (what) *stands in the path of sinners*, nor (what) *sits in the seat of the scornful*; but *his delight is in the law of the LORD*, and in His law he meditates day and night.

The father now anticipates the pointed questions to be hurled at him from his son. They are probably the same questions he threw in anger at his own father: "Why can't I spend time with my friends? You don't even know them. You know nothing about them. You're trying to control who I hang around with. They're my friends and you can't choose my friends for me!"

In reality, the father does know all about his son's friends and what will inevitably happen to them. He also knows what will happen to his own young son if he continues down this path in a relationship with them. How does he know? Because he believes the Word of God and the warnings given. He has seen firsthand, all through his life, the pain and suffering that have come upon those who went their own way, and shipwrecked their lives, while running from the truth. He knows. He's seen. He's been there. And it breaks his heart to imagine the same thing happening to his own son.

> **Proverbs 1:16-18** - For their feet *run* (to run swiftly, quickly, to hurry)[10] *to evil* (what is wicked,

malignant, hurtful, bad in a moral and ethical sense)[11], and they *make haste* (are anxious, hurried)[12] to *shed blood.* Surely, in vain the net is spread in the sight of any bird; but they lie in wait for (what) *their own blood,* they lurk secretly for (what) *their own lives.*

Evil is always self-destructive.

Galatians 6:7-8 - Do not be deceived, God is not mocked; for (condition) *whatever a man sows,* (result) *that he will also reap.* For he who sows to his flesh will of the flesh reap corruption, but he who sows to the Spirit will of the Spirit reap everlasting life.

Scripture teaches this truth: All who are swift to do evil and live unlike the Lord Who created them will ruin and destroy their own lives. They will sow to their flesh, causing them to reap corruption, death and despair— not only in this life, but in the life to come. In contrast, if they sow to the Spirit, as the father is admonishing his young son to do, they will reap peace, joy, love and everlasting life. There are only two roads, and only two choices. Jesus said that one leads to life, while the other leads to destruction (Matt. 7:13-14).

"Which will it be, my son?" the father asks. "Which road will you choose?"

Which will it be for you?

Just so we don't fall prey to the deception we talked about in the beginning (the "evil company corrupts good habits or morals, character" thing), the father leaves us with one final, global truth that applies to all mankind.

Proverbs 1:19 - So are the ways of *everyone* (the whole, everything, each, all, the entire, without exception, including you and me)[13] who is *greedy* (to gain wrongfully or by unrighteous violence, to cut off, to break off, to be covetous)[14] for *gain* (profit gained with selfish goals or motives in mind)[15]; *it* (the greed for gain) *takes away* (seizes, captures, to carry off as plunder, to snatch away)[16] *the life* (soul, self, desire, mind, emotion, passion)[17] of its owners.

The love for money consumes those who lust for it, like an uncontrollable, raging fire that devours all that's in its path. Unfortunately, the love for money is the hallmark and centerpiece of our society. It becomes our idol, our passion, and the standard by which we measure our own value and self-worth.

"I make more than this guy. Therefore, I'm a better man."
"I can take a better vacation than you. Therefore, I'm a better man."
"I have nicer clothes, a bigger house, and a brand new car. Therefore, I'm a better man."

In whose eyes are you deemed a better man? Yours? Probably. But you are certainly not better in the eyes of the Lord.

1 Samuel 16:7 - "The LORD does not see as man sees; for man looks at the outward appearance, but the LORD looks at the heart."

Along with our drive to be a better man, at least in our own eyes, we'll soon find ourselves willing to sacrifice our marriage, our time with our children, and even our love of our Lord for just a little more money. We are so quick to forget the sobering warning from the Lord.

> **1 Timothy 6:9-10** - But those who desire to be *rich* (wealthy) fall into temptation and a snare, and into many foolish and harmful lusts which drown men in destruction and perdition. (why) For the *love of money* (covetousness) is a root of all kinds of evil, for which some have strayed from the faith in their greediness, and pierced themselves through with many sorrows.

"Don't let it happen to you, my son," the father would say.

How Much is Enough?

One final thought. The first American billionaire, John D. Rockefeller was once asked, "How much money is enough?" He replied, quite transparently, "Just a little bit more." Or, "I really don't know. But for some reason, the millions of dollars I already have don't make me feel good about myself. So I guess a little bit more will help. Just a little bit more."

Isn't that sad?

True joy and purpose come from the "fear of the Lord." After all, the "fear of the Lord is the beginning of knowledge" (Prov. 1:7). This wonderful knowledge is the blessed knowledge of the Holy One and His ways.

Nothing compares with knowing Him.

Getting Serious

1. Have you ever been tempted by peer pressure? Have you ever changed your behavior just to fit in with friends you thought you needed in order to feel good about yourself? What was the end result of that temptation? How did it work out for you in the long run?

2. Which of the personal, *felt-need* temptations we looked at allure or tempt you the most? Is it the need for acceptance and belonging? Maybe it's greed, the lust for more money, and the happiness you think money can buy. Could it be your need for companionship and the fear of being alone? Which of these temptations hit you where it hurts the most?

3. Do you ever think the warnings from Scripture don't apply to you and your life? Maybe they were meant for someone not quite as mature, wise or smart as you?

4. When was the last time God spoke to you through His Word? What was that experience like? How often does it happen? Why don't you think it happens more than it does? Is there anything you can do to help God speak to you more?

5. On a scale from 1 to 10, how would you rate God's wisdom in your life right now and in your decision making process? What was it yesterday? Are you growing in the wisdom of God? If not, why not?

Next Step Challenge

Use your Bible to revisit Proverbs 1:11-19. Read and look carefully at the various ways sin and the world are tempting the young man, and how he is in danger of being deceived. Then, for each verse and warning, find another Scripture that adds support to the warning from Proverbs.

For example, when the father addresses the son's deceptive belief that he can sin without suffering the consequences of his sin, we find the following supporting truth:

> **Hebrews 3:12-13** - Beware, brethren, lest there be in any of you an evil heart of unbelief in departing from the living God; but exhort one another daily, while it is called "Today," lest any of you be hardened through the deceitfulness of sin.

Furthermore, when the young man is deceived by peer pressure into thinking that he must measure up to the standards of others in order to be accepted and feel good about himself, we find another supporting truth:

> **Galatians 1:10** - For do I now persuade men, or God? Or do I seek to please men? For if I still pleased men, I would not be a bondservant of Christ.

For each of the warnings in this chapter, find another supporting truth from the Scriptures to support what you've read in Proverbs. Take some time with this and search the Scriptures, both Old and New Testament, on your own. Ask the Lord for help and guidance. After all this, ask yourself the following questions. Be honest and transparent.

What have you learned about the true purpose and meaning of the book of Proverbs?

How will you let what you've learned change your life from this point forward?

Notes:

1. Zodhiates, S. (2000). The complete word study dictionary: New Testament (p. 1166). Chattanooga, TN: AMG Publishers.
2. Ibid., 809-810.
3. Ibid., 1039.
4. Ibid., 1442-1443.
5. Ibid., 1482.
6. Ibid., 708-709.
7. Baker, W., & Carpenter, E. E. (2003). The complete word study dictionary: Old Testament (p. 329). Chattanooga, TN: AMG Publishers.
8. Ibid., 929.
9. Ibid., 2.
10. Ibid., 1043.
11. Ibid., 1062-1063.
12. Ibid., 577.
13. Ibid., 506.
14. Ibid., 155-156.
15. Ibid., 156.
16. Ibid., 554-555.
17. Ibid., 746.

DAY SEVENTEEN

The Inevitability of Temptation

My son, if sinners entice you,

Do not consent.

Proverbs 1:10

IN THE CHURCH TODAY, especially in the West, we peddle the gospel of Jesus Christ— the "good news" as it is known— yet conspicuously fail to tell our young, trusting converts the "bad news" that comes along with the total package of salvation. The "bad news" is that right now, as a believer, as a Christian, as one redeemed by the sacrifice of Christ, you have an enemy. Your enemy is powerful, numerous and well-equipped. He's an experienced, battle-hardened veteran ready to fulfill his evil mission for your life. His mission is to "steal, and to kill, and to destroy" you and all that Christ has done for you (John 10:10).

Satan, our enemy, works tirelessly, 24/7 to accomplish his task.

The neglected truth of the gospel is this: Once someone passes from death to life, once they've been delivered "from the power of darkness and conveyed into the kingdom of the Son of His love" (Col. 1:13), a huge bull's eye is painted on their chest. Satan then invites and directs all the evil in the world to come and test the new child of God.

This reality should not surprise anyone who knows the Scriptures. God's Word promises us that "all who desire to live godly in Christ Jesus will suffer persecution" (2 Tim. 3:12). "Beloved, do not think it strange concerning the fiery trial which is to try you, as though some strange thing happened to you" (1 Peter 4:12). Jesus said, "If the world hates you, you know that it hated Me before it hated you" (John 15:18) and because "I chose you out of the world, therefore the world hates you" (John 15:19). Jesus continues by assuring us that we will face persecution and suffering. "If they persecuted Me, they will also persecute you" (John 15:20). When these times of testing come "rejoice and be exceedingly glad, for great is your reward in heaven" (Matt. 5:12).

Did the world persecute Jesus? The answer is obvious. They persecuted Him to His death. Did the world try to entice Him to sin, to falter, and to fail in His mission to offer Himself as a sacrifice for our sins (Heb. 7:27)? Absolutely. The world enticed Him to fall continually. Daily, in fact. From His temptation in the wilderness (Matt. 4:1-11) to the angry shouts at the cross to save Himself (Luke 23:37), Jesus was enticed.

Jesus was enticed to sin so much that the book of Hebrews states, without question, that He was "in all points tempted as we are, yet without sin" (Heb. 4:15). In other words, whatever you and I face regarding temptation— the allurement, the enticement, the almost irresistible draw to sin, lust and pride, Jesus was also tempted in the same way, and much more so, yet without sin. The

One who walked in our shoes and did not consent to sin is our perfect example of the Christian life we are to live in Him.

The Inevitability of Temptation

In Proverbs 1:10 we again see the loving father giving his naive, impressionable young son sage advice on how to live righteously in the fallen world that is the home of our enemy. His advice shows the inevitability of temptation. The power behind temptation is nothing more than the cruel reality of our life in a world that we are no longer a part of (John 17:16). Scripture teaches us the way through temptation and shows us the choices we must make to live above the fold of sin.

> **Proverbs 1:10** - My son, if sinners entice you, do not consent.

The advice begins with the personal words we see repeated over and over again in Proverbs: "My son." These words are both personal and loving. They are coming from a father who desperately wants to mature his young son before he faces the temptations and enticements that come to all people who live in this fallen, evil world. The father knows what his son will soon face. The father has been where the son is soon to walk, so he implores the son he loves to listen to the "instruction of your father, and do not forsake the law of your mother" (Prov. 1:8).

The message of the father is simple and direct. "If sinners entice you, do not consent." The message begins with the word *if*. Unlike its usage today, *if* does not primarily mean a conditional phrase or clause. It's not referring to something that might happen someday to somebody, but probably not today and certainly not to you. It means "since or because" or "when or whenever" and implies a condition that's capable and expected of being fulfilled regularly, at any moment.[1] So it is with the temptation to sin.

For the believer, temptation is a fact of life that we face every day. There's no escape from temptation and no way around it. Temptation should be something we expect and embrace, not something we fear. Even our Lord was tempted and overcame the temptation by the Word of God— and so can we.

Look who's doing the enticing and tempting? The word is *sinners.* It doesn't mean just anyone who occasionally sins. No, this word refers to those who are "habitual sinners, those abandoned to sin, and especially those, in this context, who make robbery and bloodshed a profession."[2] It describes those who, by their very actions, are under the wrath and judgment of God.

Don't be misled. Sinners are not just creepy old men lurking under a street light, living in the shadows, looking for someone to draw away and entice into sin. They're not always the nameless and faceless people behind porn websites who entice you with alluring pictures to simply "click" and enter into their fantasy world of sin. It's not always the strangers, the ones you really don't know, or the ones who live in anonymity that are your biggest threat.

Your greatest temptation, and your greatest enticement to sin can come from members of your own family, those in your own home, or from your closest friend. Misery and sin love company and blood is not always thicker than water. Even those closest to you can try to lead you astray. Just ask Abel about his brother Cain. Or ask Joseph about his jealous brothers. Think about what great harm they did to both him, and their father, Jacob— all because of their pride. Then there's Job and his faithless wife and friends who seemed committed to the task of trying to destroy Job's faith and trust in God. There's also the family of Jesus who mocked Him by claiming "He is out of His mind" (Mark 3:21) when He spoke the words of God to them and others.

None of this should surprise us. Jesus promised a division among friends and family, solely because of faith in Him. He went so far as to say:

> **Matthew 10:34-36** - "Do not think that I came to bring peace on earth. I did not come to bring peace but a sword. (how) For I have come to 'set a man against his father, a daughter against her mother, and a daughter-in-law against her mother-in-law'; and a man's enemies will be those of his own household."

As bad as all this sounds, our greatest enticement to sin will often come from where we least expect it— our own flesh.

Enticement Comes from Within

James reveals to us that often our enticement to sin comes from within. He speaks about how we're to respond when we find ourselves suffering in the midst of a great trial or a seemingly irresistible urge to sin. How do we overcome in the middle of the battle? How did we get into this no-man's land in the first place and whose fault is it anyway? Where does the blame lie?

First, note the blessing promised to a man who is tried in the fire of temptation and enticement, yet stands strong and is found approved, or whose actions are found pleasing and acceptable to the Lord.

James 1:12 - Blessed is the man who (what) *endures* (remains under, to persevere, sustain, to bear bravely and calmly)[3] *temptation* (a trial of one's fidelity, integrity, virtue, to put to the test) [4]; for when he has been *approved* (tried and found pleasing and acceptable, to be tried as metals by fire and be purified)[5], he will receive (what) the crown of life which the Lord has promised to those who love Him.

Then, notice how our natural tendency is to point the finger and find someone to blame for our trials— someone other than ourselves. Unfortunately, that Someone is often God. But James puts temptation into proper perspective for us. God *never* tempts us to sin and God is *never* the source of our sinful desires or lusts.

James 1:13 - Let no one say when he is tempted, "I am tempted by God"; (why) for God cannot be tempted by evil, nor (what) *does He Himself tempt anyone.*

Someone is tempting us to sin, we reason. It's got to be someone's fault when we find ourselves in the midst of a great trial. Somebody has to take the blame. Someone did this to us. We demand to know who that someone is.

The answer to our quest for blame is quite revealing.

James 1:14 - But *each one* (you and me) *is tempted* (how) when he is *drawn away by* (what) *his own desires and enticed* (to bait, entrap, beguile, deceive).

Our temptation comes from within— from the very core of our fallen nature. It's our flesh, our pride, the insistent demanding of our own rights, our rebellion, our insolence, and our lusts and desires that can plunge us into the darkness and despair of sin. And just how great is the darkness and despair of sin?

> **James 1:15** - Then, when *desire* has conceived, it gives birth to *sin*; and sin, when it is full-grown, brings forth *death*.

The Scriptures reveal that *desire* naturally leads to *sin*, and sin will ultimately bring forth *death*. It really doesn't get much darker than death.

Since we often think these things will never happen to us, James adds the following admonition:

> **James 1:16** - Do not be *deceived*, my beloved brethren.

That's right, do not be deceived into believing these verses don't apply to you and your situation. Don't think that you're too spiritual or mature to fall for some inward temptation. Don't count on never being foolish enough to be drawn away by your "own desires and enticed" (James 1:14). Don't be deceived into thinking it will only happen to others, and not to you.

To "Entice"

Finally, Proverbs states that *sinners* will *entice* us and, when that happens, we are told not to consent (Prov. 1:10). What does *entice* mean? Why did the Lord choose this particular word to describe temptation?

The Greek word translated *entice* means "to be spacious or wide open, to deceive, to persuade, to seduce."[6] The word describes those who are simple, naive, gullible and easily overcome by sin. It's the same word used to describe Delilah as she *enticed* Samson to explain the source of his great strength (Judges 16:6). Proverbs 16:29 tells how a "violent man *entices* his neighbor" in order to lead "him in a way that is not good." The word speaks of persuasion and deception in order to get one's own way among those who are naive and easily manipulated.

Persuasion and deception can come from the *outside* (through others) as well as the *inside* (within ourselves). As the comic character Pogo once said, "We have met the enemy, and he is us." This is also true when we are enticed to sin.

My Son, the father implores, *if* (when) *sinners entice* and persuade *you* into sin, your only hope and deliverance in the midst of temptation is to commit to your response beforehand. *Do not consent.*

Do Not Consent

What does the father mean when he says to his son, "Do not consent"? What does it look like in real, practical terms?

That's something we will look at next time.

Getting Serious

1. What things do you struggle with in your spiritual life? What sins or carnal mindsets always seem to get the best of you? Are there some areas in your life you have tried to change, but you failed so many times that you gave up and quit trying?
2. Can you see any common thread in your struggles with temptation? Is there any particular area in your life that is more susceptible to sin than others?
3. Do you believe it's possible to have victory over your sin? Or have you resigned yourself to the roller-coaster life of sin (ask for forgiveness, and then sin again)?
4. If you believe victory over your sin is possible, are you experiencing that victory today? If so, what is it like? How did it happen? Can you share the steps you've taken to achieve your victory? If you haven't experienced victory over your sin, do you know why? Is the failure with Him? Or is the failure with you?
5. On a scale from 1 to 10, how would you rate God's wisdom in your life right now and in your decision making process? What was it yesterday? Are you growing in the wisdom of God? If not, why not?

Next Step Challenge

The Hebrew word for "entice" is *pathah*, and means "to deceive, to persuade, to be gullible."[7] It describes a person who is simple, naive and easy prey to sin. With your Bible, look up the various uses of the word *entice* in the Old Testament and see if you can grasp a deeper understanding of what the Lord is saying to us in Proverbs. Study to see how the word is used elsewhere in His Word.

For example:

Exodus 22:16
Deuteronomy 11:16
2 Samuel 3:25
1 Kings 22:20-21
Job 31:27
Proverbs 24:28; 25:15
Jeremiah 20:10
Hosea 2:14

What do the various uses of *pathah* show you regarding its use in Proverbs 1:10? What does "entice" really mean? How has your understanding and appreciation of the word changed?

Do you have a deeper desire to study the Word of God word by word? Do you see the importance of every word given to us by our Lord? Has this compelled you to become a student of His Word, in a much deeper sense, in order to "present yourself approved to God, a worker who does not need to be ashamed, rightly dividing the word of truth" (2 Tim. 2:15)?

If so, what are you prepared to do about it?

Notes:

1. Baker, W., & Carpenter, E. E. (2003). The complete word study dictionary: Old Testament (pp. 66-67). Chattanooga, TN: AMG Publishers.
2. Ibid., 329.
3. Zodhiates, S. (2000). The complete word study dictionary: New Testament (pp. 1424-1425). Chattanooga, TN: AMG Publishers.
4. Ibid., 1136.
5. Ibid., 476.
6. Ibid., 404.
7. Baker, 929.

DAY EIGHTEEN

Just Say "No!"

My son, if sinners entice you,
Do not consent.
Proverbs 1:10

THE NIKE SLOGAN, "JUST DO IT", was reportedly coined in 1988 in an advertising agency meeting. It was inspired, according to Dan Wieden, by convicted killer Gary Gilmore's last words before he was executed by a firing squad at the Utah State Prison on January 17, 1977. "Just Do It" has been the most recognized and successful trademark in the history of athletic footwear.

The loving father in Proverbs 1:10 is also coining a phrase for his naive and inexperienced young son in regards to sin. Just like the Nike slogan, the father's words are crisp, pointed and direct. "My son, if sinners entice you, Do Not Consent." To put it in Nike terminology: Just Don't Do It.

Don't Give In. Don't Give Up. Do Not Consent. Just Don't Do It. Just Say "No!"

The Sovereignty of God

For decades, nearly a century in fact, there has been much debate regarding the sovereignty of God versus the free will of man. The debate has basically centered on the question: "Where does the sovereignty of God end and the free will of man begin?" Or, "How can God be sovereign in all things yet give free will to men?" Since we see only what fallen men can see, sovereignty and free will appear contradictory. From our perspective they are polar opposites. They are like different sides of different coins.

This is never more true than in trying to understand the doctrine of salvation.

Does God, as the Scriptures teach, choose "us in Him before the foundation of the world" (Eph. 1:4) and then give us faith to place in Him, based on His choice of us, and not our choice of Him? In other words, was Jesus truthful when He said "you did not choose Me, but I chose you and appointed you that you should go and bear fruit, and that your fruit should remain" (John 15:16)? Or do we, by carefully examining the claims of Christ, freely choose Him as our Savior and, in doing so, secure our salvation by our own free will? Does the gift of salvation come by our choice of Him or by His choice of us? If it is the latter, what is God's choice based on? Our merits? Our future potential? Our standing in the community? Or maybe it's our ability to comprehend all the facets of the atonement and therefore choose, based on our own inherent intellect, to believe His claims about Himself and place our faith in Him?

That all sounds good. But none of those reasons are *true*, no matter how *true* they might seem to us.

The Scriptures teach that God is sovereign in all things (Psalm 115:3), including our salvation. God alone is *omniscient* (all knowing), *omnipresent* (all present) and *omnipotent* (all powerful). He can do whatever He pleases, without having to give an account to anyone, especially you or me. God says, "I will have mercy on whomever I will have mercy, and I will have compassion on whomever I will have compassion" (Rom. 9:15). It's His choice and His will. It's not based on any inherent merit of the ones who are blessed to be the recipients of His gift of grace. Romans 9:16 continues, "So then it is not of him who wills, nor of him who runs, but of God who shows mercy." That's right. It's God and God alone who is sovereign in salvation, and not the other way around.

Some of us, with a fallen sense of justice and fair-play, will reason and ask, "Why does He still find fault? For who has resisted His will?" (Rom. 9:19). Or, "why does God hold us accountable for not believing in Him when He is the one who chooses those who believe in Him in the first place? That doesn't seem fair."

But God never answers this question in Scripture. Instead, He chastises us for even asking it. The very question itself impugns the character of the Father who, in His sovereignty, chose us in Him in the first place.

> **Romans 9:19-21** - You will say to me then, "Why does He still find fault? For who has resisted His will?" But indeed, O man, who are you to reply against God? Will the thing formed say to him who formed it, "Why have you made me like this?"

> Does not the potter have power over the clay,
> from the same lump to make one vessel for honor
> and another for dishonor?

The Scriptures teach that God's choice of us in Him was based on "His good pleasure" (Eph. 1:5, 9), and nothing more. He chose us because He wanted to and because He could. For a reason we can't fully understand, it somehow pleased Him to choose us. This fact alone should be reason enough to surrender our lives to Him in wonder and awe.

Salvation is a subject that we'll continue to discuss. For now, let's look at our free will in regards to sanctification. To put it another way, let's discover how our free will determines what we do with the gift of salvation once we possess it.

Salvation and Sanctification

There comes a time in our spiritual lives when it's all free will. Everything becomes our choice. The choices we make will either bring honor or disrepute to the name of Christ. That time is *after* salvation, *after* the Holy Spirit has come to reside within us, and *after* we've become "a new creation" in Christ (2 Cor. 5:17).

The name of that process is called sanctification. It's the process whereby we learn to grow and live holy and perfect, just as our "Father in heaven is perfect" (Matt. 5:48).

After salvation our free will kicks in to the point that sanctification is almost always according to our choices, our decisions, and our free will. God has saved us and has gifted us with Himself, in the Person of the Holy Spirit, who empowers us with the ability to walk godly in Christ. Because of this ability and power, He expects us to live righteously. We now bring Him glory by choosing to walk in the Spirit, and by not fulfilling the lust of the flesh (Gal. 5:16).

We see time and time again in Scripture how our free will is involved with the process of sanctification. For example:

> **Romans 12:1-2** - I beseech *you* therefore, brethren, by the mercies of God, that *you* present *your* bodies a living sacrifice, holy, acceptable to God, which is *your* reasonable service. And (*you*) do not be conformed to this world, but (*you*) be transformed by the renewing of your mind, that *you* may prove what is that good and acceptable and perfect will of God.

> **James 4:**7 - Therefore (*you*) submit to God. (*you*) Resist the devil and he will flee from *you*.

> **2 Timothy 2:22** - (*You*) Flee also youthful lusts; but (*you*) pursue righteousness, faith, love, peace with those who call on the Lord out of a pure heart.

> **Joshua 24:15** - "And if it seems evil to you to serve the LORD, (*you*) choose for *yourselves* this day whom *you* will serve, whether the gods which your fathers served that were on the other side of the River, or the gods of the Amorites, in whose land you dwell. But as for me and my house, we will serve the LORD."

As seen in these passages, there is an individual, personal, free-will choice each of us must make in order to live according to the Spirit within us, and not according to our fallen flesh.

Do Not Consent

Proverbs 1:10 says, "If sinners entice you" or if sinners try to draw you away and compel you to sin, your immediate, knee-jerk, emphatic response is to stand firm and say, "No". You do not consent. You do not give in. You do not go along with them. With steeled determination and resolve, you dig in your heels and say, "No". You remain steadfast, solid and unmovable. You defiantly refuse to yield one inch, no matter the consequence or cost. You do not speak one word, except "No".

Your answer is always, "No".

You walk in the Spirit and not according to the flesh (Gal. 5:16; Rom. 8:1). You decide to follow the Lord in all things. You do what Christ commands (Luke 6:46).

This is what the church today calls mature salvation or being "sold out" to Jesus. Biblically, it's just the normal, everyday life of a believer. There is nothing out of the ordinary or noteworthy about it. Based on Scripture, the default position for any Christian is to not give in to sin under any circumstance— regardless of what our friends, family, or fellow church members might say otherwise.

The bottom line is that you and I have to be the ones that do not consent. We have to take responsibility for our spiritual life and actions. We have to take responsibility for the time we spend on the trinkets and toys of this culture versus the time we spend with the Lord. We've got to be the ones who take responsibility for the words that come out of our mouths, the things we see with our eyes, and what we allow our hands to touch. It's our responsibility to live according to the words and example of Jesus, who gave His life for us.

Jesus said, "But why do you call Me 'Lord, Lord,' and not do the things which I say?" (Luke 6:46).

When we're enticed by our flesh, the world, our lust, our pride, or by everything in us that wants to do evil, how do we respond? Do we wait for God to grab us by the arm and forcefully remove us from our temptation while we kick and scream like a spoiled child who can't get what he wants? Or do we take responsibility for our own actions? No matter how painful it might be, we must not consent or give in to sin.

This is what makes a believer in Christ pleasing unto the Lord. It's saying "no" to us, and "yes" to Him in all things. It's dying to self and living for Christ.

> **Galatians 2:20** - I have been (what) *crucified with Christ*; (to what extent) *it is no longer I who live, but Christ lives in me*; and the life which I now live in the flesh I live (how) *by faith in the Son of God*, who (1) *loved me* and (2) *gave Himself for me*.

> **Matthew 16:24-25** - Then Jesus said to His disciples, "If anyone desires to come after Me, let him (1) *deny himself*, and (2) *take up his cross*, and (3) *follow Me*. For whoever desires to save his life will lose it, but whoever loses his life for My sake will find it."

Remember, "When sinners entice you, do not consent" (Prov. 1:10). Do not consent like Eve did in the garden when she plunged all mankind into sin (Gen. 3:4-6). Do not consent like David did while looking lustfully at a woman who was the wife of a close friend (2 Sam. 11:2-4). Do not consent to pride like Moses did before he forfeited his chance to enter the Promised Land (Num. 20:7-12).

Instead, be like Joseph who did not consent to sin, even when enticed by the wife of Potiphar (Gen 39:7-12). Be like Job, who was severely tried and tested, as much as any man, yet did not sinfully blame God for his suffering (Job 1:22, 2:10). We cannot be forced to sin and then try to blame our sin on God (James 1:14).

It's our choice. The responsibility is in our hands.

As Martin Luther said, "Here I stand, I can do no other."

I pray this can also be said of me and you and the church today.

Getting Serious

1. When was the last time you gave into sin? Did it just come upon you and catch you off guard? Or did you have the opportunity to say, "No", but chose to do otherwise?
2. What prompted your decision? What was the result? Did the sin satisfy? Was it all worth it in the end? Were there any residual effects to your giving in to temptation? Were there any blessings that you lost?
3. How long was it before you asked for forgiveness? Did you ask immediately? Did you wait a while? Did it take a day or two? Or did it take longer?
4. If you did wait to ask the Lord for forgiveness, why was that? What was your motivation? What were you thinking? What were you trying to gain? Were you, in some way, trying to punish yourself for your sin? Did you think that maybe the Lord wouldn't forgive you until some time had passed? Was there another reason for your delay?
5. On a scale from 1 to 10, how would you rate God's wisdom in your life right now and in your decision making process? What was it yesterday? Are you growing in the wisdom of God? If not, why not?

Next Step Challenge

Use your Bible to read more about the children of God who yielded to the temptation to sin, versus the ones who stayed firm and did not consent. What can you learn from their stories of success and failure?

Eve - Read Genesis 3.
Moses - Read Numbers 20:7-12.
David - Read 2 Samuel 11:1-12:25.
Job - Read Job 1:6-2:10.
Joseph - Read Genesis 39.

Do you see yourself in any of these accounts? What would you have done differently if you found yourself in the same situation, or had faced the same temptation?

What are you doing now when temptation comes your way?

DAY NINETEEN

Stupid Is as Stupid Does

"How long, you simple ones, will you love simplicity?
For scorners delight in their scorning, and fools hate knowledge."
Proverbs 1:22

IN THE LAST CHAPTER WE HEARD THE WISE, strong, and direct words of the loving father to his impressionable son commanding him, and us, to stand firm in the face of temptation. The father simply said, "Do not consent" (Prov. 1:10). That was it. There was nothing more to add. There was no margin for error in what the father said. There was no grading on the curve, no second chances, and no consolation prize for just showing up.

His command and impeccable wisdom were summarized in just three blunt words: "Do Not Consent!"

But what if we do? What happens when the son, like each of us, decides to go his own way and reject the wise words of his father? What happens when we know the truth of God and His commands, but still choose to shake our fist in the face of our Creator and demand independence, autonomy, and our perceived right to rule our own life? What happens when *we* chafe under the mantel of "servant of God", or "slave of God", and insist that *we* are independent contractors who will give God only what *we* think He deserves when *we* decide to give it?

What happens then?

The Call of Wisdom

By the time we come to Proverbs 1:20, we note a change in the text. Wisdom is now personified as a woman: a virtuous, godly woman that stands in stark contrast to the adulterous woman we are warned about in Proverbs 7:10-21. We see this woman (wisdom herself) calling out to those who have not heeded the "do not consent" command of the father and are walking dangerously close to the edge of a cliff. She calls out to them at the top of her voice, pleading with them, imploring them, and literally begging them to watch their step and to beware of the grave danger below.

She cries out to them wherever they are, in the open concourses, at the city gates, and in the public square. She works tirelessly and refuses rest until they hear her voice and heed her warning. She will do whatever is necessary to get her message out to the young man, and to people like us, who are being led astray.

> **Proverbs 1:20-21** - *Wisdom calls aloud* (cries out, to be overcome)[1] *outside* (without, on the street); *she* (wisdom) *raises her voice in the open squares* (in the broad or open places, a public square).[2] *She cries out*

(calls out, declares, to summon)[3] *in the chief concourses* (where people are heard, a place of public proclamation), *at the openings of the gates in the city* (where the leaders of the city transact official business) *she speaks her words.*

This woman, who is wisdom personified, proclaims her warning everywhere people can be found. We see her in the marketplace, on Wall Street, and in the aisles of the local Wal-Mart warning everyone of the danger of rejecting the wisdom of God and embracing sin. She's on the streets of Washington DC, and she's in the center of our neighborhood cul-de-sac, crying out her message to all who will hear.

This is what she calls to all who will listen:

> **Proverbs 1:22** - "How long, you simple ones, will you love simplicity?"

How Long?

How much longer will you continue in your foolish ways? How long until you finally learn from your own mistakes? How long are you going to beat your head against the wall? Please tell me! How long?

The Hebrew word translated both "simple ones" and "simplicity" is *petiy* and means "foolish, inexperienced, profoundly naive or simpleminded."[4] It describes a person who is dumb— *real* dumb. Not dumb in the mentally retarded sense, but dumb in the prideful, boastful, un-teachable, "I already know everything" sense. It describes someone who refuses to learn from the past and is doomed, by their own arrogance, to repeat their folly over and over again.

Wisdom asks each of us the same question: "How long, you foolish, simpleminded, stupid ones, will you love your stupidity? How long, you fools, will you be enamored in your folly?"

The crux of the question is this: When will you learn? Or, will you *ever* learn?

When will you take seriously the warnings of the Father and the commands of Scripture? When will you learn to be submissive and just obey what the Lord says? When will you get tired of repeating the same mistakes and suffering the same consequences over and over again? When will you finally get bored with the trinkets of this world and the fleeting pleasures of this life and jump, head first, into the abundant life Jesus promised (John 10:10)? I mean, haven't you learned anything yet? Are you really that dense?

Stupid Is as Stupid Does

As Forrest Gump would say, "Stupid is as stupid does."

The church often resembles a confused young man who puts quarter after quarter into a drink machine and never gets a drink. How long would you do that? How much time and money would you waste before you slapped yourself on the forehead and said, "You know, I'd better stop. This machine isn't going to give me what I want, no matter how hard I try. It's stupid to keep wasting my money."

You'd be right. It is pretty stupid.

"Stupid is as stupid does."

We see the warnings of the Lord ignored all the time in the church today, as if obedience is no longer valued. One marriage fails due to hidden character flaws that are left unaddressed, and before you know it, the next marriage fails for the same reason. The recently, twice-divorced father of two asks, "Why do I always have so much trouble when it comes to relationships? Why won't any of them work out?"

"Stupid is as stupid does."

A young woman sees all her friends getting married. Instead of waiting for the Lord, or listening to the loving, wise counsel of her parents, she rushes headlong into a relationship with a guy who shares none of her values. Before you know it, she painfully discovers that "bad company corrupts good character (1 Cor. 15:33 NIV)." Now alone, used, and feeling great shame, the young woman asks herself, "Why didn't I listen to the voices of those who loved me or the truth of the Word of God? Why did I allow all of this hurt and heartache to happen to me?"

"Stupid is as stupid does."

A young father works 80 hours a week to make a name for himself in the company. All the while he justifies his pride and ambition as "sacrificing for his family." Every night his children say their prayers without him and every morning his wife eats her breakfast alone. Then one day the young father finds himself strangely drawn to his attractive secretary who seems to understand him more than his tired, busy, diaper-changing wife. Before he knows it, the young father has violated his marriage vows, committed adultery, and brought upon himself the curse revealed in Proverbs 7:21-23:

> With her enticing speech she caused him to yield,
> with her flattering lips she seduced him.
> Immediately he went after her, as an ox goes to the

slaughter, or as a fool to the correction of the stocks, till an arrow struck his liver.

As a bird hastens to the snare, he did not know it would cost his life.

Again, "Stupid is as stupid does."

Embrace Wisdom

The only way to stop the "stupid is as stupid does" cycle of sin and its devastating consequences is for each of us to make a clear, lifelong commitment to (1) refuse to rely on our own understanding about anything (Prov. 3:5), no matter how painful it might prove to be, and (2) clutch to the teachings and commands of Scripture as a drowning man would a life preserver. Because that's exactly what the Word of God is for us— a life preserver. To embrace it and hold it close will bring us deliverance and life. But to cast it away from us in the raging seas of this world brings only death.

So what are we to do?

The Sunday School answer is this. "I will trust in the Lord with all my heart and lean not on my own understanding. I will, in all my ways, acknowledge Him and His Word and obey what He says about everything" (Prov. 3:5-6).

Great! You get a pat on the head and a gold star by your name. Good for you. But do you really mean it? Or is this just another game we play with ourselves when we want to feel a bit more spiritual? Maybe it's more like a promise we make to the Lord when we want something from Him, hoping to "butter him up" to say *yes* to what we want Him to do?

Remember the charge from the Lord:

Proverbs 1:22 - "How long, you simple ones, will you love simplicity?"

How long will you naive, foolish, simpleminded people *love* foolish, simpleminded things? How long will you foolishly derive your self-worth from the worthless, fallen things of this world? How long will you be enamored with the same worthless, fallen things? What will it take to get you to look up and see life and purpose from the vantage point of the eternal and not the temporal? When will you choose to work for treasures in heaven and not for the stuff that rusts, fades and rots away (Matt. 6:19-21)? How long will it be before you quit thinking like the person you used to be (2 Cor. 5:17) and realize that you now have the "mind of Christ" (1 Cor. 2:16)?

How long will you allow this insanity to go on?

How long, you simple ones, will you love simplicity?

Don't you think it's about time to embrace wisdom for all it is? Don't you think Jesus needs to be more to you than He is right now? Don't you think it's time to change?

If you're ready for change, head on over to the final section of this book. Let's give serious thought to what the life of wisdom, as a follower of Christ, is all about.

Getting Serious

1. Did you ever think, from the Lord's perspective, that many of your decisions are stupid? Have you ever said to yourself, "Boy, I don't ever want to do that again"— and yet find yourself foolishly doing the very same thing, with the very same results, that you swore you would never do again?

2. Have you ever had to learn the same lesson from the Lord twice, three times, or more? Why do you think that is? Why do you think it's so hard to learn what He wants to teach you?

3. Does your inability to get victory over a sin, thought pattern or character trait sometimes make you feel stupid? Does the word "stupid" make you a bit angry? If so, why do you think that is? What other less-offensive word would you use to describe your actions?

4. What would it take for you to obey the Lord in all things? What would you have to do to truly live Proverbs 3:5-6? Is it even possible? If so, do you think the promise from the Lord is real and true and something He would grant to you?

5. On a scale from 1 to 10, how would you rate God's wisdom in your life right now and in your decision making process? What was it yesterday? Are you growing in the wisdom of God? If not, why not?

Next Step Challenge

With all honesty, make a list of the top five disastrous decisions you've made and the consequences of each. Write down what you *thought* would happen and what *really* happened. Who was hurt? What price did you pay? What were the long-term consequences of those five decisions? Are you still suffering the consequences of those decisions?

Then, with 20/20 hindsight, take out your Bible and look for the wisdom of God that would have prevented you from making those decisions, had you taken the time to look before you acted.

What verses did you find? What principles did you discover?

What lessons have you learned?

Notes:

1. Baker, W., & Carpenter, E. E. (2003). The complete word study dictionary: Old Testament (p. 1061). Chattanooga, TN: AMG Publishers.
2. Ibid., 1045.
3. Ibid., 1009-1010.
4. Ibid., 1424-1425.

PART THREE

"And if it seems evil to you to serve the LORD, choose for
yourselves this day whom you will serve, whether the gods which
your fathers served that were on the other side of the River,
or the gods of the Amorites, in whose land you dwell.
But as for me and my house, we will serve the LORD."

Joshua 24:15

"Blessed are you when they revile and persecute you, and say all
kinds of evil against you falsely for My sake.
Rejoice and be exceedingly glad, for great is your reward in
heaven, for so they persecuted the prophets who
were before you."

Matthew 5:11-12

DAY TWENTY

Not Every "Christian" Will Suffer Persecution

All who desire to live godly in Christ
will suffer persecution.
2 Timothy 3:12

IF YOU'RE CONCERNED ABOUT HOW SEVERE the persecution of Christians and the church will get in America, you're far more astute in understanding the "signs of the time" than most professing Christians today (Matt. 16:3). In America, we have adopted a "Don't Ask, Don't Tell" mindset regarding current events and how they might interrupt what we hold most dear: our vacations, our retirement, our free-time, our video games, and a false sense of security regarding our immature relationship with Christ.

Did that last phrase sting a bit? If so, it shows you're not completely anesthetized to what is happening all around us.

How dire will the persecution get? Well, that all depends on what kind of "Christian" you are and what type of church you attend.

Let me explain.

We Will Not All Be Treated Equally

Not everyone will suffer the same under the coming persecution, just like they didn't all suffer the same under Nero's reign of terror during the first century of the church. Nor did all Christians suffer the same under the persecution of the Third Reich. Dietrich Bonhoeffer, for example, was martyred for his faith on Monday, April 9, 1945. But just six days later, churches throughout Germany met in their own buildings for Sunday worship. They were not harassed or afflicted at all by the Nazis who murdered Bonhoeffer earlier that week.

How could that be? Why did one group of professing Christians suffer persecution at the hands of the Nazis, while another group freely worshiped with the permission and approval of the Third Reich? How was that possible?

More recently, twelve Christian missionaries, including the 12 year old son of a ministry team leader, were crucified and beheaded near Aleppo, Syria for not renouncing their faith and for not converting to Islam. If they had caved into their fears, as some did, and renounced the Jesus they loved, they would be alive today. Instead, they rejoiced "that they were counted worthy to suffer shame for His name" (Acts 5:41) and died a horrific death. For those twelve, it was more important to obey God, rather than man (Acts 5:29). They unmistakably proved that "the world was not worthy" of them (Heb. 11:38).

Again, there were two groups of professing Christians. One group renounced Jesus and lived. The other remained faithful to Him and died. The two groups were not treated equally. The severity of their persecution was contingent upon their commitment to Christ. Throughout church history it has always been that way, and it always will be.

Soon, in our own country, we will see pastors and true believers punished for preaching and teaching the whole Word of God, especially the politically incorrect passages from Romans 1:26-27 that deal with the sin of homosexuality. You heard right: the *sin* of homosexuality. Those who refuse to compromise the authority of God's Word, in favor of politically protected and government sanctioned sin, will suffer persecution. They will be fined for their faith in the One Who does not change (Mal. 3:6). Many will lose their positions, their life savings, their businesses, and even their homes because of their unwavering faith. They will be marginalized, vilified, mocked, ridiculed, threatened and sued. Some will be arrested, charged with a hate crime, and imprisoned for their faith.

Just like in Bonhoeffer's day, Christians will be languishing in prison for speaking truth that the culture rejects, while others will be leading or attending churches deemed "acceptable" and "tolerant" in the eyes and ears of the State and the courts.

What's the difference? What separates the two groups?

Simply this: Desire. A desire to live godly in Christ— no matter what it costs.

Those Who Desire and Those Who Don't

In 2 Timothy 3:12 the Scripture states, "All who desire to live godly in Christ will suffer persecution." Note the condition and the promise. It's one of the **if/then** conditions and promises found in Scripture. **If** you do this or meet this condition, **then** this will happen.

An **if/then** condition and promise means that **if** we do our part, **if** we meet some sort of condition or requirement the Lord has established, **then** we can have the confidence to know that God will fulfill what He has promised to do.

We see conditions and promises throughout the Scriptures.

There's the one from Romans, for example, that we often use when we share our faith with others.

> **Romans 10:9** - *If* you confess with your mouth the Lord Jesus, and (*if*) **you** believe in your heart that God has raised Him from the dead, (*then*) **you** will be saved.

When it comes to persecution, the Lord gives us another **if/then** promise.

> **2 Timothy 3:12** - All who (*if you*) desire to live godly in Christ (*then you*) will suffer persecution.

The surety of suffering is a promise from the Lord. The same promise is echoed by Jesus when He tells us to not be surprised about persecution. "If the world hates you, you know that it hated Me before it hated you" and "If they persecuted Me, they will also persecute you" (John 15:18, 20).

Let's look at the **if/then** condition and promise again.
Make it personal.

The Condition: "*All who (if you) desire* (will, wish, want, strive, make it your aim)[1] *to live* (have your existence, your mode or manner of life)[2] *godly* (devoutly, reverently, obediently)[3] *in Christ...*"

The Promise: "*(then you) will* (shall, most certainly) *suffer persecution* (distress, trouble, peril)[4]."

Not all will suffer the same. The defining characteristic of those who will be persecuted, versus those who won't, will be an innate "desire to live godly in Christ." This longing and passion to live godly in Christ, no matter the cost, is the hallmark of a committed Christian's life. It's a desire to know nothing but Jesus Christ and Him crucified (1 Cor. 2:2). To live as a committed Christian— as a *real* Christian, is to boldly acknowledge Him before kings and governors (Matt. 10:18). True commitment is to count our life as worthless, except for following Him and being faithful to what He has called us to do (Acts 20:24). After all, isn't that why He saved us in the first place?

When the darkness begins to fall and the persecution of the church becomes impossible to ignore, some church goers will have a great desire to "walk as Jesus walked" (1 John 2:6) and renounce the deeds of darkness in obedience to Him (2 Cor. 4:2). Sadly, most won't. Some will suffer for the sake of their Lord, knowing this world is not their home (Heb. 13:14), and they will be blessed to be called ambassadors of Him, the One True King (2 Cor. 5:20). Others will love their life in this world: their status, their financial security, and their ease and comfort. They will renounce their love for Jesus, in either word or deed, and will forsake their inheritance as a child of God (Rom. 8:16-17) for something far less. While real Christians are rejoicing in the privilege of suffering for the truth, just like their Lord (Acts 5:41), others will continue the pageantry and charade of being good, acceptable, tolerated "Christians".

The stark difference between these two groups will be apparent to all. Actually, it's apparent now. Can you tell the difference?

Not all so-called Christians will suffer persecution at the hands of the government or be hated by our culture. Some will live in prosperity and comfort, proudly bringing their Bibles to the approved churches (the ones that proclaim the virtue of tolerance for sin and promote a god that's created in the image of man). But some will not compromise. They will bend their knee to no one but the Lord Jesus (Rom. 14:11). They will render to Caesar what is Caesar's but they will not, under any circumstance, render unto Caesar what is God's (Matt. 22:21).[5]

In which group of the persecuted do you belong?

Are you one of those who will be persecuted for the sake of Christ because you desire, above all else, to live for Him? Or are you one of those who will persecute Jesus and His Church by feigning your loyalty to Him with false spirituality and loving your life in this fallen, perverted world more than you love the Lord?

Are you the righteous or the hypocrite? Are you one who cries out, "Blessed is He who comes in the name of the Lord!" (Matt. 21:9). Or will you, surrounded by an angry, Christ-hating mob, shout through your own apathy and indifference, "Give us Barabbas! We have no king but Caesar!"? (John 18:40, 19:15).

Which will it be?

You can't have it both ways. Persecution has a tendency of forcing those it confronts to either one side or the other.

On which side will you be?

Only those who truly belong to Christ will be willing to endure suffering and persecution. In fact, true believers will embrace the honor of suffering persecution as an opportunity to show the unbelieving world to Whom they belong.

Do you belong to Him? If so, how do you know?

Do you understand why acquiring the wisdom of God is so important, especially as we see "the Day approaching" (Heb. 10:25)?

If so, let me encourage you to take a deep breath and keep reading.

Notes:

1. Zodhiates, S. (2000). The complete word study dictionary: New Testament (pp. 727-728). Chattanooga, TN: AMG Publishers.
2. Ibid., 697-698.
3. Ibid., 685.
4. Ibid., 473.
5. This statement comes from Dr. James Dobson in his response to the June 26, 2015 Obergefell v. Hodges Supreme Court Ruling regarding gay marriage. http://drjamesdobson.org/specials/the-supreme-court-and-the-american-people

DAY TWENTY-ONE

No Wheelbarrow, No Salvation

"Not everyone who says to Me, 'Lord, Lord,'
shall enter the kingdom of heaven,
but he who does the will of My Father in heaven."
Matthew 7:21

ONE OF THE GREATEST TIGHTROPE walkers the world
has ever seen was a man named Charles Blondin— or, as he was
known internationally, the Great Blondin. Charles Blondin was
born on February 28, 1824 and rose to international fame by
being the first person to tightrope across Niagara Falls. He was a
master showman, highly skilled at his craft, and gifted with a
unique, riveting flair for the dramatic. For the better part of three
decades he entertained huge, mesmerized audiences on both sides
of the Atlantic.[1]

His greatest feat took place on June 30, 1859, when he became
the first man to cross the great Niagara Gorge.

Today we call it Niagara Falls.

On that day, over 25,000 people gathered on both the American and Canadian sides of the Falls to watch the Great Blondin attempt the impossible. He was to walk on a thin rope, only 2 inches in diameter, and made entirely of hemp. The rope was stretched 1,100 feet across the gorge, and was suspended 160 feet above the raging river— all without any safety net or harness. One small slip, one slight loss of concentration and focus, one unforeseen gust of wind, and the Great Blondin would fall 16 stories to his death.

The crowd watched with nervous anticipation as he slowly, carefully, step by step, one foot in front of the other, made his way along the swaying rope, crossing a distance of over three football fields in 23 minutes. When he finally reached the Canadian side, the crowd burst into a roar of triumphant applause.

But the Great Blondin wasn't finished.

Over the next few days he walked across Niagara Falls many times, and each time with increasing dramatic theatrics. Today's walk had to be greater than yesterday's show. One time he walked across blindfolded. Another time he used wooden stilts. He crossed again while wearing shackles and another while wearing a gunny sack. Blondin crossed riding a bicycle. He crossed in the dark. One time he carried a stove on his back and cooked and ate an omelet over the middle of the Falls. With each crossing, he pushed the limit of what the audience thought he could do. Each time they responded in praise and adulation for the Great Blondin. They believed he could do anything on a tightrope. "Nothing," they said, "was too difficult for the Great Blondin!"

One day he walked across Niagara Falls while pushing a wooden wheelbarrow. The audience enthusiastically cheered. Then he placed 350 pounds of cement in the wheelbarrow and made the return trip. When he arrived back at the American side, the crowds broke into thunderous applause.

Looking at a man who seemed to be cheering the loudest, the Great Blondin asked him, "Do you believe that I am able to carry a man across in this wheelbarrow?" The man eagerly proclaimed, "Yes! I believe you can. In fact, I *know* you can!" Smiling, the Great Blondin replied, "Then get in."

The man refused.

Blondin turned and addressed the watching crowd. "Do you believe I am able to carry a man across the Falls in this wheelbarrow?" They all responded loudly, "Yes!" Again, Blondin asked, "Which one of you will get into the wheelbarrow and let me push him across?"

They all refused.

No one was willing to get into the wheelbarrow. No one was willing to place their life in the hands of the Great Blondin. No one was willing to have him push them across the Falls, although they all firmly believed he could do it. They'd just seen him push 350 pounds of cement across in the same wheelbarrow, but refused to get into the wheelbarrow themselves.

What's the disconnect between faith and trust? What's the difference between simple belief in something or someone and trusting them with your very life?

It's the difference between saving faith and non-saving faith. It's the difference between true salvation and being deceived into thinking you belong to Christ. It's the difference between the narrow road to eternal life and the wide road of destruction that Jesus warned about (Matt. 7:13-14). It's the difference between living for eternity in heaven with Christ or a horrid eternity of dark torment in hell.

It's the difference between life and death, light and darkness, heaven and hell.

It's the most important issue in life.

The Difference Between Belief and Surrender

Are you one of the ones that believe the Great Blondin can do what you've seen him do? Or, do you refuse to place your life in his hands? Do you refuse to act on your belief and get into the wheelbarrow?

Eternal life with Christ does not come from simple, cognitive belief. Just believing is not enough. You might believe in Jesus. You might even believe that Jesus is the Son of God and that He died on the cross for your sins. You might believe He rose from the dead, ascended into heaven, and is now seated at the right hand of the Father. You might even go so far as to believe Jesus will someday come again to defeat Satan and bring forth eternal righteousness. Although you might believe that day is coming soon, none of your belief alone leads to salvation. None.

Satan and the demons believe the same things about Jesus (James 2:19). In fact, Satan doesn't just believe. He *knows* Jesus is the Son of God. Satan *knows* He rose from the dead. He *knows* Jesus is coming soon to judge the living and the dead and that thought makes him tremble (2 Tim 4:1). Still, Satan defiantly refuses to bend his knee to the Lordship of Christ (Rom. 10:9, 14:11). That's why Satan will spend eternity in "everlasting fire prepared for the devil and his angels" (Matt. 25:41).

What about you? Do you believe like Satan believes?

It doesn't have to be that way. Your life now and your future eternity can be different. But please know that your time is running out.

Head knowledge (mental assent) is not enough for salvation. Believing the Great Blondin can take a person across Niagara Falls in a wheelbarrow is not enough— unless you are willing to be that person. You've got to be willing to get into the wheelbarrow. You can't watch from the sidelines and think you're saved. You've got to place your faith, your trust, and your entire life into the hands of the Lord Jesus for salvation to take place. You've got to surrender every part of your will to Him.

Jesus' terms are non-negotiable: It's all or nothing. Jesus gives you all that He is for all that you are. It's called the Great Exchange: His Perfect Life for Your Broken Life. You give Him all of your life, including the good and the bad, and He comes to live in you permanently and forever.

You must die for Him to live. It's called being born again and it's the most amazing thing this side of heaven (John 3:3-8).

It's Not What We Say, But What We Do

If you only claim to be a Christian, you're probably pretty mad right now that I would be so bold as to "judge" you and your spiritual life. If you have a Facebook page, you would probably put "Follower of Jesus" or "Christian" or something like that as your religion tag. But look at your life. Look at the fruits of your years of living. How much has any eternal value or significance? How much of what you do every day gives glory to the God you claim to serve? How many of your actions and deeds are good, holy, just and righteous? Jesus called them spiritual "fruits" that the Holy Spirit gives to those who belong to Him (Matt. 7:16-20). Jesus said, "Not everyone who *says* to Me, 'Lord, Lord,' shall enter the kingdom of heaven, but he who *does* the will of My Father in heaven" (Matt. 7:21).

It's not those who *say* they believe in Jesus that will enter the kingdom of heaven. It's those who *do* the will of the Father. It's not our words, no matter how sincere and well meaning they might be. It's the spiritual fruits, given only by the Holy Spirit, that are the true proof of genuine salvation.

So examine yourself. Are there spiritual fruits manifested in your life? If not, be honest with yourself. You know you're not a Christian. If you will let yourself think beyond the immediate, you know you're not going to heaven, and that breaks my heart.

We, the church, have failed you many times and haven't lived the Christ-like example we should before you. I ask for your forgiveness for our failures. I also ask you to not judge Jesus by me or any other Christian. We're a poor example of who He is. He's all love and, as you know, we're not. He's gracious and forgiving, and we're not. He's more than I can describe and more than you'll ever need or want— but you must put your trust and your entire life into His hands. Let Him change you from the person you are into His own image— the person He created you to be. He doesn't want to make you better.

He wants to make you new.

Just Ask

All you have to do is ask. Then, get into the wheelbarrow and let Him take you wherever He wants. You must put your entire life into His hands and hold nothing back.

My dream and prayer is for you to know and experience Jesus for who He really is— not who you think He is or who the church has portrayed Him to be. He's far more than anything you can imagine (Eph. 3:20-21). My prayer for you has been the same as

Paul's prayer for those he loved. He said the same thing that I want to say to you:

> **Ephesians 1:17-21** - That the God of our Lord Jesus Christ, the Father of glory, may give to you the spirit of wisdom and revelation in the knowledge of Him, the eyes of your understanding being enlightened; that you may know what is the hope of His calling, what are the riches of the glory of His inheritance in the saints, and what is the exceeding greatness of His power toward us who believe, according to the working of His mighty power which He worked in Christ when He raised Him from the dead and seated Him at His right hand in the heavenly places, far above all principality and power and might and dominion, and every name that is named, not only in this age but also in that which is to come.

Don't wait. Get into the wheelbarrow. Give everything to Him. Ask Him today. Beg Him to be the Lord of your life. Then watch the transforming power of His Spirit change everything about you so that the rest of your life will be a blessing to many.

Notes:

1. Abbot, Karen, "The Daredevil of Niagara Falls."
    http://www.smithsonianmag.com/history/the-daredevil-of-niagara-falls-
    110492884/ (October 18, 2011).

SOME FINAL THOUGHTS

The LORD looks down from heaven upon the children of men,
to see if there are any who understand, who seek God.

Psalm 14:2

Then you will call upon Me and go and pray to Me,
and I will listen to you.
And you will seek Me and find Me,
when you search for Me with all your heart.

Jeremiah 29:12-13

DAY TWENTY-TWO

What Do You Value Most?

*"Do not lay up for yourselves treasures on earth, where moth and
rust destroy and where thieves break in and steal;
but lay up for yourselves treasures in heaven, where neither moth
nor rust destroys and where thieves do not break in and steal.
For where your treasure is, there your heart will be also."*
Matthew 6:19-21

WE'VE SPENT QUITE A BIT OF TIME together looking at
the book of Proverbs, with the goal of obtaining the wisdom of
God that we so desperately need. We need as much wisdom as
possible as we begin to see our culture implode into the craziness
of transgender bathroom wars, and all that comes with a society
on the verge of chaos.

I'd like to end our time together with a personal plea. I'd like
to ask you to join me in begging our Lord to reveal Himself to us,
to His church, in a way that will change all of our lives, no matter
what happens.

Show Me Your Glory

Let me share my heart with you this way.

Often I find myself asking the Lord to reveal Himself to me. Like Moses, I continually plead, "God, show me Your glory (Ex. 33:18), or at least let me experience a little of what the early church did back in the book of Acts. Lord, give me something. Anything. Give me a glimpse— just a tiny taste— of Your awe, Your power and Your majesty."

I really don't know what I am expecting God to do. Maybe a flash of light, like Peter and John saw when Jesus was transfigured before them (Matt. 17:2). Maybe a chance to see the Spirit of God move in the wind and fire, like Elijah saw at the mouth of the cave (1 Kings 19:11-12). Maybe I'd like to feel the foundation of my house shaken by the power of God, like it did when the early church prayed (Acts 4:31). I don't really know. My hope is for something memorable. Something out of the ordinary.

But definitely something more than this.

Have you ever felt the same way? Have you compared the life of the church, portrayed in the book of Acts, to your own life and wondered what went wrong? What's missing? If you have, did it drive you to the Scriptures? Or did it drive you to a church service that made you feel electrified with pulsating music and long, drawn out periods of spiritual aerobics? You know what I mean. There are churches that try to imitate what they think the Spirit feels like by manipulating the flesh. We've all seen it done and we know how superficial it is at best. It's a bad copy of the real thing. A counterfeit. A mirage. Smoke and mirrors.

Which brings us back to the Scriptures.

"Lord, is there somewhere in Your Word that will show us how to know You more? Is there a key passage that will unlock the secret of getting close to You and satisfy our desire for more of You? Lord, will you please help us out?"

His answer is always, "Yes."

The Word of God is full of passages that show us what is necessary to have intimate fellowship with Him. Many of them have to do with living right and striving for holiness, which is not a popular topic in today's Laodicean church.

Before you tackle graduate level sanctification, such as taking every thought captive to the obedience of Christ (2 Cor. 10:5), walking by the Spirit and not according to the flesh (Gal. 5:16), and not being conformed to the image of this world (Rom. 12:2), you need to take a step back and examine your level of commitment to living a life of intimacy with the Lord. It's not something to be taken lightly. It's a radical change of existence. You will die daily to yourself in order for Christ to live larger and stronger in you. It's a trade: All of you for all that He is. It will be an adventure of great heights and deep valleys, of pain and hardship and failure. But it's also an adventure of breathtaking seasons of sheer bliss. "Is the pain and hardship worth it?" Absolutely! But there's a price to be paid to hear God speak and a price to understanding the knowledge and wisdom of God.

Are you willing to pay the price?

If so, let's finish our time together with some Scriptures that speak of what it takes to know the wisdom and knowledge of our God. These verses tell us how intense our desire should be for more of Him.

All or Nothing

Proverbs 2 begins this way, with an implied **if/you**:

> **Proverbs 2:1-3** - My son, *if* (a conditional clause)
> you receive (snatch, hold, get) my words, and (*if*
> *you*) treasure (hide, store up) my commands (not
> suggestions) within you, so that you incline (heed,
> hearken, attend) your ear to wisdom, and apply
> (stretch out, extend) your heart to understanding;
> Yes, *if* (a conditional clause) you cry out (call,
> summon) for discernment, and (*if you*) lift up
> your voice for understanding,

Can you feel the rising level of intensity in these words? It's
more than simple mental assent or wishful thinking. There's a
sense of tremendous urgency, helplessness, and reckless
abandonment in these words. It's as if the Lord tells us to seek
discernment and understanding like a drowning man seeks one
more breath. We must want it more than anything else, and more
than life itself.

> **Proverbs 2:4** - *If* (a conditional clause) you seek
> her (wisdom, discernment, understanding, the
> knowledge of God) as silver, and (*if you*) search
> for her as for hidden treasures;

We're to seek, desire and crave the wisdom and knowledge of
God more than all the treasures we spend our lives trying to
accumulate. We must want God's wisdom and knowledge more
than gold and silver, more than comfort and ease, and far more

than our own pleasure. We must seek for the wisdom of God like the man in search of fine pearls (Matt. 13:46), like the woman with the lost coin (Luke 15:8-9), and like the man who found the treasure in a field (Matt. 13:44). We must be willing to sell all that we have to possess the wisdom of God, the knowledge of God, and the hallowed presence of the Lord God Almighty.

Nothing else really matters.

> **Proverbs 2:5** - *Then* (the result of all the previous *ifs*) you will understand the fear (reverence, awe, terror) of the Lord, and find the knowledge of God.

Adveho quis may.
Come what may.

Choose Life

"I call heaven and earth as witnesses today against you,
that I have set before you life and death,
blessing and cursing; therefore choose life,
that both you and your descendants may live;
that you may love the LORD your God,
that you may obey His voice,
and that you may cling to Him,
for He is your life and the length of your days."

Deuteronomy 30:19-20a

About the Author

Steve McCranie has been a pastor for over thirty years and currently serves at a church in North Carolina. He can usually be found hanging out at his blog, LeavingLaodicea.com.

To share his concern about the state of the church and to warn of the coming persecution it will face, he created a podcast called Coming Darkness. The purpose of this podcast is to help the church acquire the necessary wisdom from God's Word in order to know how to navigate the troubling days ahead. You can find his podcast at ComingDarkness.com.

Steve McCranie is married to his best friend, Karen, and together they have five children and eleven grandchildren (so far).

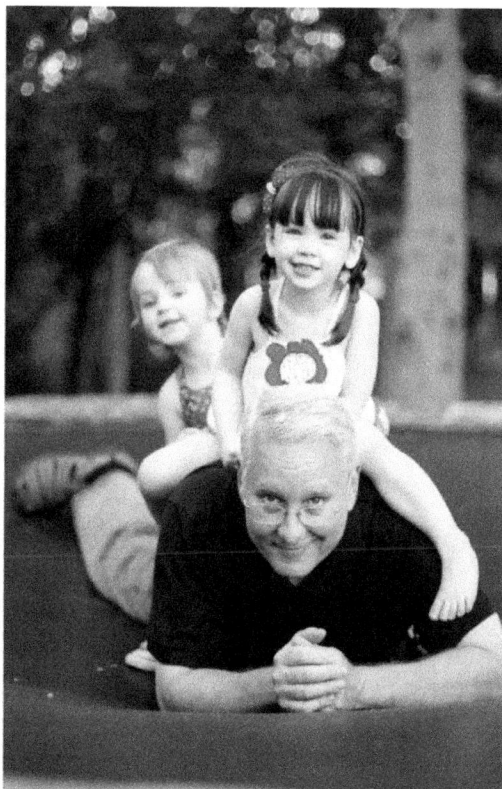

Steve McCranie with two of his eleven grandchildren having some
fun on the backyard trampoline.